About the author

Tom lives in Staffordshire in the West Midlands, in the UK. After leaving school, he went to college to study carpentry and followed in his brother's and father's footsteps, working as a carpenter in the refurbishment industry. After seven years, Tom left the building trade to turn a hobby into a career and successfully became a personal trainer. It was during the Covid-19 outbreak and the subsequent lockdown that Tom decided to use the extra time and turn his hand to writing. In a time of turmoil for us all, he wanted to use this time to try to help people and hopefully put a positive spin on this negative time. With his writing, Tom wishes to motivate and inspire those in a dark place, to show that we all have the power to achieve anything we desire as long as we believe in ourselves.

COMPRESSION OF DEPRESSION

TOM WILKINS

COMPRESSION OF DEPRESSION

Vanguard Press

A CIP catalogue record for this title is
available from the British Library.

ISBN 978 1 80016 285 3

*Vanguard Press is an imprint of
Pegasus Elliot MacKenzie Publishers Ltd.*
www.pegasuspublishers.com

First Published in 2022

**Vanguard Press
Sheraton House Castle Park
Cambridge England**

Printed & Bound in Great Britain

Dedication

Obviously throughout this book there have been many challenging times, some I'm sure you can relate to. But the more difficult processes can be, the bigger and better the rewards can be when you make your way through them. I'm a man who likes to have his independence however it can also, from time to time, make things just as demanding. While there are times when it's down to you to roll up your sleeves, put in a shift and get the job done, sometimes luck will play a factor. I'm lucky enough to be a person who has some absolutely incredible human beings around me, who support me and always have my back. A huge thank you to the family and friends that I have in my life. I would walk through fire for you all... because I know you would all do the same for me.

Chapter 1
Nice to Meet You; I'm Tom

So as I mentioned in the introduction, I'm Tom Wilkins and, at the time of writing, I am twenty-eight years old. I was born in Leamington Spa and lived in Warwick before moving to a small village called Stonnall in Staffordshire when I was nine. I have lived in Staffordshire ever since, moving to Chasetown in Burntwood when I was twelve. My parents divorced when I was twenty-two, and I moved in with my dad and future stepmother in Lichfield. After not quite seeing eye to eye with her, I then moved in with my mum when I was twenty-six, and I'm still currently living with her in Rugeley. My two older brothers also live here in Rugeley and are both married with children. Ben is the eldest and has a two-year-old daughter called Olivia, and Joe is the middle brother with three boys. There's James, who is six, Harry, who is three and Charlie, who is one.

Throughout our lives, I feel we have been a very working-class family. Even with changing primary schools, I feel a lot of the friends that I have grown up with were middle class or had more available to them. Not all of them were middle class, of course, and it wasn't a bad thing that they were middle class, but I just feel that life was slightly more difficult for my brothers and me growing up. Our secondary school was in Lichfield, which is a nice city to be in, and I'd love to live there one day, but I lived in Chasetown at the time. Houses were much cheaper there, but I lived away from all of my friends. Even the kids I got the school bus with lived two or three miles away. Lots of my friends were dropped off at school and in nicer, newer cars than we could afford.

In year 10, we were given lunch passes which meant we could go out of school for lunch. The closest place we could go to was Morrisons — just down the road from school. A lot of the kids I walked down with had at least a fiver a day to get lunch, whereas I had about that much to last the week. I remember when I saw friends at the weekends or went to their houses, a lot of them lived in detached houses with multiple cars on the drive. Again, not all of my friends were middle class, but it just showed that most of them had more things available to them as their parents were better off financially. It isn't their fault that my family is working class or that we lived in Chasetown; I just want to let you know a few things about myself before we delve deeper into my mental health story.

Neither of my brothers or I went to university once we had left school. I can only think of a handful of people that I went to school with that didn't go to university either. It's not that we weren't clever enough, just that we wouldn't have had the finances to allow us to. Ben was the only one who went to sixth form. He started working at a local Goodyear factory not far from the Chasetown house before a strict talking to from Dad about how little he was making got him into college to become an electrician. He was very tech-savvy with games and computers growing up, and my grandfather owns a plumbing and electrical company, where Ben got an apprenticeship. My dad is a carpenter and, after working with him in summer holidays and half terms, Joe got an apprenticeship with him and went to college part time. They have worked for different companies since and in higher positions, but Ben is still an electrician, and Joe is still a carpenter.

When I left school, I had absolutely no idea what I wanted to do. I knew I wanted to do something physical and manual but had given no thought whatsoever to what I wanted to do as a career. Still being a teenager, all I had thought about was passing my GCSEs, getting a job, then seeing where life went. The closest thing to a career that I had thought about was as a bass player, starting a band with friends and seeing how far we could go. I never really gave any serious thought to what I would want to do as a profession or what I needed to do to get there. When it came to a career, I just wanted something that I didn't think was embarrassing, such as a binman or a cleaner (being a teen, everything was about my image) and something that paid well. As I went through my school years, I wasn't one for taking risks. I'm a big rugby fan but didn't join the school team until year 10; I always look back to the start of secondary school in year 7 and think what could have been if I had joined then. I wasn't really a sporty person at the time, but the only real reason I didn't join then was because I didn't know anyone else who was trying out. This mentality also drove me to make my eventual decision on a career. I did the same as Joe and ended up being an apprentice carpenter with my dad. I went to the same college that Joe did too, which was Stafford College. With him already going and knowing the lecturers, I had some idea of what to expect.

At this time, it proved that it wasn't necessarily what you knew but who you knew. I passed the college course and went on to be a carpenter full time for five years. Now having gotten my first full-time job, I was paying my parents rent; this was, and still is, £25 a week. I had also reached the legal drinking age, so pretty much every weekend, I was out getting hammered with my mates. As many school friends were still at university and had moved out of the Midlands, I'd started making new friends, a lot of whom were also working class and similar to myself. An average night out was about £50 for me as we were usually in Lichfield, and taxis cost about £15. As I was earning more than most, I'd often splash the cash… especially if I had a crush, as I was a hopeless and often clueless romantic. The point of this information is that I wasn't really saving or putting anything away. As an apprentice, I was earning £4 an hour, and this rose to £6.50 after completing my apprenticeship. The only times that I would save were if we had planned a trip somewhere — a lads' holiday or going to a festival. I saved for driving lessons and eventually got my first car, but my insurance was through the roof. I was buying my own food, paying my parents rent and, like I said, was paying my car insurance, so the only disposable income I had was spent on nights out.

Through school and my teen years, I thought life had its own distinct path and things needed to be done by certain times or that things needed to happen at certain times. In school, I had a mix of male and female friends, and lots were getting into relationships. I remember thinking that if I wasn't in a long-term relationship by the time I had left school, that it would never happen. Obviously, now I know this isn't the case, but it led to me asking everyone and anyone if they'd go out with me. As mentioned earlier, after reaching eighteen, I was in pubs a lot. The main reason was that I wanted to have a laugh and a good time but also because it was the best place to meet girls. Being the hopeless romantic I was, I spent loads on drinks and treating girls to all sorts, which meant less money that I was saving. I wasn't thinking about saving for a place of my own because I just wanted a relationship so badly. I also thought that the older I got and more experienced at work I got, that I'd get pay rises in the future, so could think about houses later in life.

As I approached my early twenties, I had been, and was still, in the frame of mind that if I wanted a pay rise, then I'd have to work really hard to get one. I hoped that the harder I worked, it would eventually show and one of the site or contract managers would take notice and offer a raise. Unfortunately, in the construction industry, and no doubt in many other industries, this isn't the case. All our managers cared about was the work getting done and done on time. They didn't care too much about quality, and I was still just a young worker to them. It wasn't until one of my co-worker's weddings that I got the advice that I needed. The guy getting married was the owner of the company's nephew, and a lot of the company's staff were there, including the senior contracts manager. He was rather shy as he introduced his rather tipsy wife to us. Me being the youngest meant she thought I was adorable and was jokingly (or so I thought) telling me not to let him push me around. She followed up by shouting, "Don't kill yourself for him. If you want a raise, then just go up and ask him for one; he doesn't own you."

This advice helped me so much in later life and taught me that if there's something you want, then go and get it. One of my most commonly used phrases is, "If you don't ask, you don't get."

Unfortunately for me, in the company I was working for, the senior contracts manager only cared about themself and, unsurprisingly, I wasn't given a raise.

When I turned twenty-two, I looked into becoming a labourer and doing agency work. The company I was already working for was just taking the mick. We were always working away, the jobs were getting worse, and new site managers were inexperienced and useless. We were treated like dirt and, to the managers, we were just tools to use to get the job done — no appreciation whatsoever. Being a labourer meant I'd be working locally, I wouldn't be spending money on tools or maintaining them, and if there was a job I didn't like, then I could just change jobs or agencies. As a labourer, I worked on a lot of new housing developments. A lot of the time, I was tidying and prepping areas for the different trades, taking in the deliveries and locking up the houses. Luckily, with my previous carpentry experience, I was able to do small carpentry jobs and snagging as well. Snagging is basically a checklist of things that need doing after a job is done — a door handle may be on the wrong way or a cupboard door on the wrong side. This put me ahead of other labourers and made me seem more valuable and productive to the site I would be working on.

At this point, my finances hadn't really improved too much. When I wasn't at work, I was at the gym. I love doing weights and strength training, it's a great way to ease stress, and I'd always wanted to be muscular. I remember as a kid in the late nineties watching wrestling and watching Schwarzenegger films such as *Predator*, *Running Man*, and *Commando* with my dad. Seeing all these muscle-bound guys in these films and wrestling was an inspiration for me. The gym was and still is my main hobby.

A friend I used to go with to the gym worked in retail and had started going to college part time to become a personal trainer. Again, like the school rugby team, I didn't have the confidence to think I'd be able to do it or afford it. Luckily for me, my girlfriend at the time was very supportive and found a further education company called The Training Room. With them, I could do the learning from home so I could carry on working, and the tuition fees could be paid monthly. I signed up immediately and started thinking about being able to turn a hobby into a career and leaving the construction industry for good.

Like I've said, my finances hadn't improved much since becoming a labourer, and the monthly PT tuition fees weren't leaving me with much either, so I got myself an overdraft. It was a double-edged sword because I'd always said to live for the moment. This often meant if there was a chance to do something exciting, then I'd do it, even if that meant going into and over my overdraft. The bank also gave me a credit card at the same time, saying I could use little bits of the card limit to get back into my overdraft if I had gone over that limit. I'd get the money from my next wage to pay off the credit card and pay off any fees. Problem was that this was getting more and more regular, and I couldn't remember the last time my account was in positive figures. I had opened another bank account to deal with this, but the same thing kept happening. There were overdraft fees, late fees and also the monthly payments on my personal training course. My credit card was at its limit, and I was getting charged penalties. Stupidly, I had kept the same frame of mind that the older I got, the more I'd earn. I also kept thinking that I'd be raking it in once I became a personal trainer. So to pay off the penalties, I got more credit cards with smaller limits so I didn't get into more debt. But obviously, by this point, I had already gone too far and was already over £5000 in debt.

To try to solve this issue, I had looked into getting a loan with a guarantor. I had asked Ben if he could help me and be my guarantor, but he told me that he wouldn't be able to. He convinced me to have a talk with him and my dad as they'd both had difficulties with debt in the past. I let them know who I owed, how much to each of them I owed and how much each payment was. They recommended an IVA (Individual Voluntary Arrangement) to me. This basically meant I told the IVA company how much money I had coming in and going out, and they would speak to all the companies I owed money to. They all agreed on a figure that I could afford to pay weekly so that the companies were getting paid whilst I was still able to pay bills and living costs without getting into more trouble. This was probably one of the best decisions I've ever made in my life. My finances were finally under control, and I was in a much better position.

Now that I was worrying less about money, I could focus more on my personal training studies. Fourteen months after initially signing up for the course, I had finally passed with flying colours. I was now a level 2 qualified fitness instructor and a level 3 qualified personal trainer. I also passed several CPD courses, which allowed me to teach a range of fitness classes, including spin classes, gym-based boxing and circuit training. I got my first PT job at Fitness First in Walsall Wood, and the future was looking amazing for me.

To train clients at Fitness First, I needed to pay rent to use the facilities there. When I first started, rather than paying rent, I would work shifts over the week. This would give me the chance to get to know the members and start gaining clients there. From what I can recall, I'd start at ten hours a week with no rent, then five hours with £50 rent to finally no more shift work and £100 rent. This was based on the idea that my client base would grow as my shift hours decreased, and my earnings would grow as the rent costs increased. Due to this, I still had to work as a labourer, and I did my Fitness First shifts in the evening. Because I was working in the daytime, I struggled to get clients and was burning myself out with how much I was working: forty-five hours a week labouring, ten hours working at the gym, plus around six hours a week doing my own workouts. I was getting stuck in a vicious cycle and wasn't making enough money to leave the building trade. With the rent I was paying at the gym, it felt as if I had to pay to work there.

Luckily for me, a friend of mine had taken notice of this. A friend of his had just bought a personal training franchise called Train Learn Go. The basis of this firm is that people would sign up, and the trainer would train them in their own homes. Trainers would get a selection of equipment and drive to each client as and when you both agreed. The major plus of this was that there were no rental payments for the equipment. This was perfect for me, and yet again, after leaving Fitness First, my finances were settling down. My client base was picking up, and with only pay coming in, I was finally saving enough to be able to leave the building trade. I remember my last day on site, putting my high-visibility vest into my hard hat, slinging it into a skip and walking to my car with more swagger than an eighties pimp. I was singing and dancing in the car all the way home; this was definitely the best day of my life.

As I progressed with my PT career, I found that self-employment was a lot harder than it seemed. I was getting by, but yet again, I was finding that it was only enough to live on. Friends kept mentioning that I should take a break or have a holiday but didn't understand that in self-employment, holiday pay doesn't exist. There were times that I was getting stressed and worrying, but I still loved the work that I did. It was so rewarding to help people and finally get the appreciation I'd wanted for years. Like I said before, I was getting by, but business was stuck at the same level. Personal training is an expensive business, and not everyone can make time for it with work and children to take care of. I was starting to break down and worry more often. By this point, I was around twenty-five going on twenty-six, and I remember every time I'd go on social media, people around my age were buying houses, getting engaged and having children. I hadn't done any of these things and was feeling like a failure. I would tell myself, and friends would tell me as well, that I'd taken a massive leap of faith in changing careers, doing something that lots of people don't do and that I should be proud of myself for taking that chance and succeeding in doing so.

To save money, I started to work out at home rather than go to a gym. I've got lots of weights and other bits of equipment so I wouldn't be losing out too much. I remember one session in particular I was doing at home and, not for the first time, I broke down into tears. This time it meant more, as this was the first time I'd started to think to myself, that maybe I was depressed. I had realised that previous breakdowns weren't just one-offs, and certain issues weren't going away. I wasn't happy in life. I remember having a chat with a friend of mine about work and the difficulties I was having. Things like not earning enough and continually working without time off.

While my name is Tom, ever since primary school, and still to this day, everyone knows me as Squidy; I even use it as my name on Facebook. But it was during this chat that my friend said he had noticed the hard times I was going through, and in one of the hardest hitting phrases I've been told, he said, "You're not being the same Squidy that we all know."

It was because of this that I recorded a video of myself and put it on Facebook, telling everyone that I thought I might have depression. I told people about my situation and how I felt like I was failing in life compared to what others were doing with weddings, houses and travelling the world. How my relationships averaged a couple of months because they were usually just helping me to get over a crush. Or how I hadn't been on holiday for over three years and had never left Europe. The embarrassment I felt, that I was twenty-six and had never had a place of my own to live. It was the first time I'd ever opened up like that, and I was fighting to try to hold back the tears and my emotions.

I recorded the video because I knew it would be easier than talking to a friend or family member face to face. While I appreciate these people, by recording a video, no one could interrupt, and they would listen to everything I was saying. Plus, it's easier to get everything out because, unlike those close to you, a camera won't get emotional during the conversation and stop you from getting the words out. I'm not having a go at friends or family; I'm just sharing a method that helped me to get all of my words and feelings out into the open. I feel this is a major step for anyone who is going through these similar kinds of feelings. I remember after posting it online, the feedback I got was incredible. There were several people who I hadn't spoken to for years, offering me help and support. This reassured me that lots of people go through this type of thing and reminded me of what a successful person I am. It felt like an incredible burden had been lifted. To help keep me going, I would watch motivational videos online, and I even wrote out a set of goals that I wanted to achieve to keep me motivated.

I felt better for opening up about my feelings but, unfortunately, work wasn't really improving. There were good and bad times, but around late spring 2019, things had been getting worse. We just couldn't figure out what was happening. We had made lots of improvements that were successful in previous months. Anytime we lost clients, we would be signing up new ones to replace them, but it was just getting harder. There were several weeks that I was struggling to make triple figures in terms of pay. By the summer, I had decided to get myself a part-time job at the weekends to try to help with my finances.

I eventually became a delivery driver for Domino's, and while it was helping me out, I felt pretty embarrassed about it. During the week, I was helping people train and lose weight; at the weekends, I was helping others to put it on. It's not exactly the job you want people knowing that you do either. I eventually got used to it, and it was making a difference but still not quite enough.

When I mentioned my circumstances, people would often ask if I'd thought about going back to carpentry. I would tell them why I hated it so much and all the positives of being a personal trainer. My brother Joe had come away from the tools and was now a project manager at the company he worked for. He had mentioned the possibility of getting me a job there, but I would tell him the same things I'd told others as to why I didn't want to go back. I kept weighing up the pros and cons of each career and put it off for as long as I could, but eventually I realised that I needed to listen to my head rather than my heart.

In what was the most difficult decision I've made in my life; I ended my career as a personal trainer and went back to carpentry.

Chapter 2
Cabin Fever

October 14, 2019, was one of the worst, if not the worst day of my life. I didn't know it on the day, but as time went by, it started to show why it was so bad. As shown in the conclusion of the previous chapter, I had now returned to the building trade and, once again, I was a carpenter. I was working for the company that my brother Joe was working for as a project manager. By this time, I had been working there for six weeks and was working on a job in Wolverhampton. I was on my way home after finishing for the day, having dropped off the apprentice I was working with. It was around four forty-five p.m., and I was in a slow queue of traffic that was approaching a roundabout. I then opened my eyes to see my mother and a paramedic talking to each other as I was lying in the back of an ambulance.

They told me that I'd had a seizure whilst I was driving. It happened as I was coming off the roundabout, so luckily, I wasn't travelling very fast. I had hit another driver, but the only damage to the cars was a dent about the size of a football just behind the headlight of my car. Joe came to the scene with my mum and had moved my car into a nearby pub car park. He explained what happened, and they allowed me to keep my car there overnight whilst I went to the hospital. Due to me being a type 1 diabetic, most of my family's thoughts were that I'd had a hypo (hypoglycaemic attack), and this is what caused the seizure.

The pancreas regulates the body's blood sugar levels, but the pancreas no longer functions properly when someone has type 1 diabetes. This can cause the blood sugar level to drop to below recommended levels, and this is what causes a hypo. Eating or drinking something sugary will return the level to normal, but if left untreated, it can lead to having a fit or seizure. The problem that I had, though, was that the paramedics didn't believe that this seizure was due to my diabetes.

It was around 6.10 p.m. when I had awoken in the ambulance. It felt as if I had just blinked — one minute I was in traffic, next I was in the ambulance. I've had hypos before, and I do get warning symptoms when they happen, things like feeling weak and shaking. Sad to say, I've also had seizures due to hypos, and they have symptoms when I regain consciousness. Often, I will have a headache, and I will temporarily lose my short-term memory. I know basic things like who I am and who others are, but sometimes I'll forget how to use things like my phone or I won't recognise a person's name or address, but it comes back after half an hour or so. With this seizure, though, there was nothing like that. Like I said, it was just as if I blinked. I got a headache later on as the day went by, but that was due to sustaining concussion in the initial collision. But when I woke in the ambulance, I felt fine, even at one point trying to get up and leave. I'd had one or two seizures like this in the past, but never whilst driving. Sadly, I'd have some in the future too, but these weren't regular or often.

I was in A&E at Stafford Hospital for several hours, and the doctors could not find any reason for what had caused the seizure. I thought it might have been down to stress or exhaustion. I'd not long been in a job where I'd gone from working around ten hours a week to forty. I was starting much earlier, which meant I was sleeping less, and I had also been a bit nervous initially as it had been so long since I had done any carpentry. They said it wasn't my diabetes causing it because my sugar levels weren't low enough after they'd tested them after the seizure. After that, I tried to use my personal training knowledge to explain that the body gets its energy from the carbohydrates we eat. These are then converted into glycogen which is the energy that then gets stored in muscle cells. The muscles obviously use energy as fuel and need this when we exercise or move. When we exercise, this causes blood sugar levels to rise. When a person with diabetes with low blood sugar levels has a seizure, this is the body's emergency reaction to get sugar levels to rise, and this may be why my sugar levels were higher than a hypo level after the seizure. Every doctor I tried to explain this to said they could see the point I was making, but it wouldn't have been the cause.

They let me go home and told me to rest. Around three days later, I had an appointment with a neurologist at Stafford Hospital, and he let me know what they intended to do to try to find the reason for these seizures. I was to have an ECG (electrocardiogram) to see if there were any underlying heart issues, an EEG (electroencephalogram) which is used to find problems related to electrical activity in the brain, and an MRI scan of my brain to look for any signs of epilepsy. He also told me that I would have to contact the DVLA and have my driving licence revoked for at least a year. Straight away, all I could think about was how I was going to get to work. But then he said that I would not be able to work until I had been given the all clear to do so. That answered that question, but then the worry turned to, *Well, how am I going to pay my bills?*

The accident had happened on a Monday. Luckily for me, I had received a call from the tax man the week before, telling me I had wrongly been on an emergency tax code and that I would be getting a tax rebate. This meant I would be receiving this whilst getting sick pay from work, so at least it wasn't all doom and gloom at the time… or so I thought. As the days went by, I started getting frustrated because I could not go out due to not being able to drive. I'd rely on my mum to give me lifts to places or to take me food shopping. I felt bad because I knew she needed fuel for work. I love being independent and doing my own thing. I managed to qualify for a medical bus pass, so I was saving some money with that and got a bit of that independence back, but it felt like I was going backwards because I knew I could drive. I was feeling like I was less, knowing that most people who go on a bus are elderly, people too young to drive or people who simply can't afford a car, or afford to learn how to drive.

Around the end of November, Joe told me that I was to have a meeting at work with our boss. At the time, I thought this was to discuss the accident and what doctors had recommended. It kind of was to a degree, but it was just a three-month review which I would have had even if I hadn't had the accident. It was the 3rd December when I had the meeting, and the main point I told them was that I had been told I couldn't work until doctors had given me the all clear to do so. My boss was very sympathetic but, unfortunately, he told me that they would have to let me go because of this. The company wouldn't be able to keep paying sick pay for an undetermined length of time. The main reason, though, was that as the reason for this particular type of seizure was currently unknown, that meant I didn't know how to treat them, which meant I wouldn't be able to tell colleagues what they'd need to do to treat one if one happened, whereas I know how to treat diabetic seizures and had told them what they'd need to do to treat those.

At the time, it was a bit of a downer, but I knew it wasn't technically my fault, nor was I being sacked for doing a bad job. I had been receiving sick pay and my tax rebate, along with holiday pay that I was still entitled to, so I was still able to pay bills. Plus, with Christmas just a couple of weeks away, it helped me pay for all my presents for others. It wasn't till around mid-January that the lack of wages really started to hit home. Once I had received my last payslip, the negative thoughts and overthinking were really playing on my mind. It had now been three months since the last day I had worked, and I was really starting to become institutionalised.

Everyone at some point will moan about going to work or after a weekend will say how they hate Mondays or dread going back to work. After the amount of time I'd been off, though, I really appreciated how important it is and not just financially. The first couple of weeks were great because I hadn't been on holiday or off for a week in over three years due to my previous difficulty with self-employment. But as weeks turned into months, it just got harder and harder. Things start to lose their attraction. Television, especially daytime TV, because it's so repetitive, becomes stale. Video games get boring after half an hour. I train and exercise regularly, but I do one to two hours; it's not something to make the day go by. Social time is cut drastically because normally when you're employed, you meet up or chat at weekends because obviously you and your friends are working in the week. But as I was feeling more isolated, I wanted to talk but remembered everyone was at work and those who weren't probably had children to deal with and look after. Sometimes, because I was in such a negative mindset, I felt as if people were ignoring me or forgetting I existed. But I had to remember that everyone else has a life of their own.

I mean no disrespect when I say this — I am a huge fan of his — but it was getting to the point where I started to understand why Heath Ledger took his own life. All this loneliness does make you lose your mind. I had been seeing a girl in the first couple of months after the crash, which initially helped me through it immensely, but sadly we ended up going our separate ways. This wasn't the reason for us splitting, but when it came to love and relationships, I was very old fashioned and tried to be a gentleman wherever possible. As I said in the previous chapter, I was more of a hopeless romantic. But now I was starting to think that I'd never get to be in a relationship for a long time now because who wants to be with someone who's living with their mother, who's unemployed and can't even drive.

Along with the feelings of being institutionalised, other problems were working their way in. I'd received my last payslip and now needed other ways to get some cash. People had mentioned little jobs such as dog walking, but I ended up getting regular work for a friend's mother. Just doing household jobs and maintaining the garden, plus she offered to pick me up and drop me off each time. This helped, but it wasn't enough to keep me going financially. I had looked into whether I could still receive some kind of sick pay from the Department for Work and Pensions. They recommended that I look into trying to get Universal Credit. I had been getting sick notes from my doctor, and as long as I kept renewing them, I would continue to receive Universal Credit. Normally, you would have regular meetings to show you were looking and applying for work, but this didn't apply to me as I was medically unfit to work.

This had been helping me, but the underlying issue for me was that I was technically on benefits. I love my independence and showing that I can look after myself, but I almost felt ashamed that I was doing so like this. I understand how much help benefits are to people who really need them, but when most people think of people on benefits, they tend to think of those who are exploiting them. They're usually stereotyped as lazy people who can't be bothered to work or think they don't have to. Most people will hate them because it's their taxes that are paying for their life. I felt embarrassed because I knew I had qualifications, knew I had a strong work ethic, and I wanted to work. I kept telling myself and had lots of others remind me that I shouldn't feel down because, technically, it wasn't my fault.

I would get some good news here and there. My ECG scan hadn't found any issues, so this led to me having a twenty-four-hour ECG scan and then later having a five-day ECG scan, which on both occasions came back all clear. The EEG scan had also come back without any issues, and the MRI scan showed no sign of epilepsy. With no issues being found, I started to look for local jobs to hopefully get me going again. The company I was with when I had the accident had offered to bring me back once I could work again, but I knew I wasn't going to take it. I had talked to my ex-girlfriend when we were together about how I'd like to possibly go into a career in mental health. Due to my experiences with my own mental health, I wanted to help others in the same way that I wanted to help others when I was a personal trainer, just with a job that was more financially reliable rather than having a career in self-employed work.

Due to her working as an occupational therapist, I got as much info from her about the NHS and looked into possibly getting a future career within it. She mentioned being a mental physiotherapist to me. I thought that would be good for me as with all my time off, I had been looking for ways to keep myself occupied. One of which was regularly putting motivational advice on Facebook to try to help others through any difficulties they were having. This then led to me making a YouTube channel dedicated to making videos of me giving help and advice to anyone about mental health in any way I could (this is also named Compression of Depression). I also had a friend from school who went on to become a physiotherapist and offered to help me if I needed it. I thought my personal trainer qualification would also be a massive help with this as well, but I knew there would be other topics I'd have to learn about. My plan was to get a job to get some money in and use that while I studied to get the qualifications that I would need.

I had started looking into warehouse jobs and eventually was offered an interview at Tesco. I went to the interview and awaited any feedback. In that same week, I also had an outpatient appointment with the neurologist at Stafford Hospital, the same one I saw in the week of the accident. I was expecting this to be a discussion about my test results and hopefully get some sort of clearance as nothing was found. He mentioned the results but then recommended doing further tests. This would be another ECG, only this time with twenty-four-hour sleep deprivation to see if that was having any effect. I wasn't too pleased to hear this as my sleeping pattern had been quite varied due to my tendency to overthink things since the crash. He then also talked about a implantable cardiac loop recorder. This is a little device that goes under the skin and records the electrical activity of the heart, a lot like an ECG but placed internally rather than externally. I was told that I'd have to wear this for three to four months. After having my interview, I asked whether I could work whilst wearing this, but it was the same news as before... no working until a clear reason for the seizures had been found.

I was absolutely devastated after hearing this. We were in February at this point, and it meant at least another three months of feeling isolated. I would try to take others' advice and try to stay positive, but there's only so much you can do. I didn't want to be someone on social media who only posted negative things and was feeling sorry for themself all the time. The problem is when you're in a depressed frame of mind, nothing is ever really the same. I'd try to motivate others, but some days I'd wake up feeling like I wanted to conquer the world, and the next, I felt like a miserable teen, wondering what's the point of anything.

These feelings of institutionalisation were really tearing me apart. As I previously said, you see the importance of work outside of the financial implications. We all have our problems or things on our minds, but at work you don't think about them because you're working — your focus is elsewhere. In the same way that when you speak to colleagues, your issues aren't the subject, and you don't think about them or let them get to you. Being alone so often was really getting to me. I've had issues with overthinking in the past, but after the crash, it was getting more frequent. As I got more fed up with doing the same old things or getting bored with things, it would happen more and more because I was alone with my thoughts. When you're suffering with anxiety or depression, this can be a very dangerous place to be.

At first, for me, it was the health issues that were making me overthink a lot after a reason couldn't be found for the seizure when I first went to A & E on the night of the crash. *What if I have epilepsy? What if there are certain things I can't do any more? What if it's a heart condition or a brain tumour? What if it's something terminal?* After I lost my job and stopped receiving payslips, the thoughts turned to my future working life. *What if I can't do a job that pays well enough? What if I can't get a job? What if I'm never able to find my own place?*

Having to get a bus everywhere and receiving benefits made me feel less of a person. It felt as if I was going backwards and failing at life. I started feeling like I was in the place I was in when I initially realised I might have depression. Thinking about feeling like I was failing at life because I wasn't as successful as others and knew I was getting further away from that level of success. I just wanted to get out of it and, unfortunately, but only for a few seconds or so each time they entered, the darkest of thoughts would also enter my brain. This was that almost cardinal sin of suicide.

I don't think I'd ever be able to do it. I could never hurt my family or friends like that. They are the biggest motivations in my life, and they keep me going. I love meeting up with friends and try to make plans as often as I can. I may often have to put a brave face on over current situations, but they take my mind off it. They remind me of what a good person I am and how well I am doing. Writing this book has probably been the best thing I've done to help me with these feelings of isolation. So often friends and family want to know how it's going and tell me how impressed they are with me that I'm trying to do something creative rather than just feeling sorry for myself. It's March 2020 as I write this section and these months have been the toughest of my life and I'm certainly not out of the darkness yet. But with all that being said, there will be better times ahead. I said it in the introduction to the book — problems are temporary. It may be at least three months till I'm working again, it might be a year, but I will get back on my feet.

Chapter 3
A Harvester of Souls

When I was in my teens, I remember there was more talk about anxiety, and I wondered how someone could suffer with severe anxiety. I always seemed to question how someone can suffer with severe anxiety. I always thought of it as a temporary feeling or emotion. I never understood that it was a sign of depression or a mental health issue at the time. It certainly wasn't as widespread as it is nowadays, but I didn't start to get a better understanding of it until I started to go through feelings of depression myself. I think the hardest thing to do when it comes to depression or anxiety is to explain it to someone who hasn't been affected by it. To get them to understand what triggers these feelings, why they make you feel as negative as you do, just to simply make them aware of these issues. By no means is it their fault that they might not understand or relate; it's like most of us understand that chemotherapy is a cancer treatment, but we have no idea of what it's like to go through unless we go through it ourselves.

One of the biggest reasons that it's so difficult for others to understand these feelings is because they are so varied. Mental health issues will have common symptoms, but these aren't the only symptoms of them. Someone with a cold will have the standard symptoms like a cough or a blocked nose, but not having these and having a sore throat doesn't mean you don't have a cold. Everyone is different, and we are all built in different ways, mentally as well as physically. What might not seem like such a problem to you could be devastating to someone else. Different people will also react differently to certain issues. Some people look for attention, someone to talk to, whilst there are some who will do the complete opposite and shut themselves away from the world.

First and foremost, though, I would not wish mental health issues upon anyone. It's a horrible place to be in. I think that they're underestimated a lot. Quite often in life, there are bad things out there, bad things that can happen. Sadly, though, I think a lot of the time (and this is definitely something I'm guilty of myself), we believe it won't happen to us. I'm not trying to scare anyone or set them into a panic, but occasionally it does. It might not even be you who is directly affected by it, but a loved one, family member, or a friend.

I imagine that the feelings of depression that I've gone through had a very similar cause to millions of other people across the globe. Far too often in this day and age, we spend our time comparing ourselves to others. I feel that the reason mental health issues have increased in the last couple of decades is also due to a huge spike in the world we call social media. Seems the way of the world at the moment is as soon as something positive happens, we need to put it online. Obviously, there is no problem with this; everyone is free to do this. But the major reason people do this, and they may not admit to it, is to see the thoughts of everyone else. How many likes a picture gets, what people will say in the comments?

Like I said, this is absolutely fine, but the issue is that some people feel like they have to compete in life, and I was very much the same. I haven't yet put a foot on the property ladder, yet I see photos of couples outside their first house with the key. Every car I have owned was used or second-hand, but I see so many pictures titled "New Car Day." I mention the couples outside their houses, but I've struggled to even stay in a long-term relationship. Again, this is by no means the fault of the people I've compared myself to, but my feelings of depression are because I feel as though I've been failing at life. It's not just a materialistic or financial issue, though. I feel sorry for the younger generations nowadays. So many celebrities are on social media now with pictures of how they're looking and what they're up to. I'm sure I'm not the only one who thinks so, but I think the youth of today are under so much pressure and even under the illusion that they should be doing all they can to look like that too.

Before social media, to see how well someone was doing, where they lived, what car they had, you had to physically go and see it with your eyes. To see where someone had been on holiday, what swimsuit they were wearing, you had to go and see them so that they could show you the photos of that holiday. With social media, though, there are hundreds of photos saved to profiles. With a click of a button, we see how others are doing and almost feel as though it's a competition. I know this isn't the way we should look at our lives, and when you look at the long term, there are often valid reasons that we haven't achieved what we want to yet. But this is one issue that can slowly creep up on you.

For me, one of the biggest reasons we develop depression or anxiety is because of a horrible feeling that we call fear. A lot of the time, it will stop us from doing things or taking a chance because we fear what might happen. We're scared that something bad that's happened before might happen again. This one feeling can have a massive effect on us if we let it. As I mentioned in the previous chapter, I'm quite an outgoing person, a bit of a clown or joker amongst friends, but when you're told that you're not the person they know any more because of how depressed you've been... it's soul-destroying. Yes, we all have things going on in life, but when it gets to a point where these issues have taken your personality, you realise what a horrible bastard fear can really be. For me, the biggest of fears is the fear of failure.

Now I feel as though you can see why I decided to call this chapter "A Harvester of Souls". This is what mental health issues can do. They can bring on so many feelings but, sadly, none of them are good. I hate to admit it, but the two main feelings I tend to experience are shame and embarrassment. Quite often they can come on at the same time as well. Feeling embarrassed when people offer me money to help out but shame when I take it because I know I need it. Feeling embarrassed that I'm living in my mum's house and ashamed that I'm the only one in the family yet to move out. I find a lot of times after days out, especially with friends, that I'll be apologising. No one got hurt, nothing bad happened; I was just being me. But again, it's that horrible little creature known as fear and this time it's simply just the fear of letting anyone down, which in turn is another form of fear of failure.

Usually, if I'm often apologising, it's because I don't want to let anybody down or because of the way I'm feeling; I think I'm not good enough for them. I doubt that I'm alone in these types of feelings. A common phrase within mental health nowadays is that you're not alone, but I feel there's a misunderstanding when it comes to this. Most people going through some form of mental anguish probably understand that they're not the only people going through something like this. But I think that because there is so much variety in mental health, they think the anguish they are going through is theirs and theirs alone. We understand that other people have anxiety and depression, but we feel that our reasons for suffering with it are different from others. Often, we don't talk about feeling alone because it's something we're ashamed to talk about. It can often embarrass us to talk to others about this kind of thing. For me, being a man, opening up and showing emotion is something we've been taught not to do as we grow up. This isn't to say that it's easier for women or they don't feel embarrassed, but it's hard to suddenly do something that you've rarely or never done.

Yet again, though, I think that it's a massive reason for this fear. A lot of times, if there is something that we don't want to do, it's down to fear. More often than not, we fear the consequences, what will happen when we have done it. We fear that if we talk to someone we know, like a friend, they may look at us differently or not feel the same way about us. If it's a family member that we open up to, we might worry that we'll upset them. Another option can be to talk to someone that we're not close to about it, a doctor, for example, but then sometimes, with this being the case, we can be afraid that maybe they won't take us seriously enough. The biggest fear that I feel people have, though, isn't one that they're necessarily aware of or one that's obvious to see. As I said at the start of the chapter, it's difficult to get others to understand what you're going through or how you feel if they haven't been through it themselves. I wouldn't be surprised if, deep down, when people think about opening up about their mental health, that this is what they fear the most. Not the fear of people understanding that they are depressed or what's causing them to feel as they do, but just not understanding what it's like to be feeling how they do.

Anxiety and depression, in my eyes, often get misconstrued and seen as a particular feeling. Throughout this chapter, there is a lot of talk about fear, but in my mind, fear is simply what I think is the cause of a lot of people's anxiety or depression. The sad thing is that when you do start to suffer with these kinds of mental health issues, there are so many different feelings and emotions that can go with it. Sometimes, the reasons for feeling depressed can be brought on by a particular event, a death, for example, or a break-up. But what surprises me a lot is how much these feelings and emotions can differ. Some days I've woken up, and I'm ready to take on the world, take on all comers, any time, any place. Whereas there are other days where I just can't be bothered to do anything, not in the mood for anything and hope that tomorrow is a different story.

More often than not, the emotions and feelings we go through when feeling depressed are going to be negative, but again they can vary so much, and this in itself is something that will knock you about. Whatever the reasons that have caused your anxiety or depression, if we get time to ourselves and start to think about it (overthinking, which is something we'll touch on later), we tend to get different perceptions about it. One day you might be angry about it, another you may feel sad about it, and if there is someone else involved, you may have seen things from their point of view. But even then, it may cause negative feelings because now you may feel bad or sorry for them, which may also cause you to feel guilty. Even as I'm sitting here writing these words, it's making me realise even more how much of an emotional rollercoaster our mental health can be.

To be someone who is suffering from anxiety or depression is simply an awful place to be. Something that can affect you in so many different ways. I'm sorry to say that it's also something that can catch you off guard or when you least expect it. If you stop and think about what it actually is, what it actually does. It's an illness that can make people feel worse about themselves; it just sounds horrific. I believe one of the worst things about it is the fact that it is still a relatively unknown world, and with fear being mentioned a lot in this chapter, the fear of the unknown is one of the greatest fears out there.

Don't get me wrong, there are a lot of treatments and ways to help depression and anxiety, but it's not just something that can be treated with a pill and then goes away for good. There's no way of knowing how long it's going to affect us or if it will ever stop affecting us. All too often, we can sometimes think that we're getting over it, but then, out of nowhere, there'll be something else to trigger it. If there's someone out there that we know that is struggling in life or with their mental health, of course we want to do all that we can to help them through it. The problem is that one of the most dangerous places for that person to be is alone in their mind.

As we know, depression is surrounded by negativity, which means anyone who's dealing with it is going to be the same. The only way is down, and every way they look at things is badly. I can relate to this far too much. I compare myself with friends and family quite a lot, and while there's nothing wrong with that, it's never going to go well in a negative mindset. While living with a parent in your late twenties might be embarrassing to most, I feel as though I'm letting my mum down, especially when my two older brothers moved out years ago. While the reasons for my current unemployment are medical and couldn't be avoided, I still often feel that I have failed in my journey to become a personal trainer. I feel that a lot of my past relationships were unsuccessful because most were just to help me get over someone I was chasing or someone else with whom I had split up with. Because I was chasing or was let go, it makes me feel as though I was never good enough. I know, for sure, that there's a ridiculous number of people out there knowing how that feels; you're probably one of them yourself as well.

The reason I mention this is, I know there are lots of good people out there, but I think we don't reassure people enough. I'm sure lots of you will say you're a good friend, and I don't doubt that, but I think we need to tell people more often just how well they're doing. I know I've mentioned it a lot in this section, but in today's social media world, it feels as though the world has gotten unnecessarily competitive. Life is rated by the number of online friends you have, how many likes your posts and pictures get. You get to judge how someone is doing based on an online profile. Unfortunately, this also gives people the thought that they can say anything to anyone from the safety of their screen, and there will not be any consequences. The world seems to be full of internet trolls, keyboard warriors, whatever you want to call them. But they seem to think that because they don't know someone, they can say whatever they want to them, good or bad.

Just because you think someone who is pretty posts too many pictures of themselves doesn't mean you can be hateful to them and judge them. Maybe they're posting pictures because, deep down, they're not happy with how they look and are looking for positive feedback. As obvious and corny as it may sound, just because someone is smiling doesn't mean they're happy. So rather than just waiting for someone to post something for us to give them feedback, why don't we make the first move? If it's someone you've known who has had troubles recently or is struggling, ask them how they're doing. Let them know that they are doing much better than they might think. Give them the reassurance that you're there for them, and they will get through the tough times. Make sure you are actually there for them, don't just comment on a negative post giving the standard, "Here if you need me x" response. Pick them up off their feet and show them how well they're doing in this moment and how well they'll do in the future. The world has become so technology-based in the last couple of decades, and I kind of feel as though this has led to us losing our human side and our sense of community. When we receive messages or texts, it's not always easy to determine how someone is feeling in that text; we don't see any real, physical expressions. So make sure when you do reassure those who need it, make sure you tell them as much as you can, and help them out of the hole they're in.

I said living with my mum often makes me feel like I'm letting her and the family down, but she says she likes having me there, much better than living all alone, and she feels safer. I said I felt like I failed at being a personal trainer, but it was my decision to call an end to it; I wasn't fired or told to stop because I wasn't good enough. There may have been relationships that I didn't want to end, but they started with someone falling in love with me, and that means someone could fall in love with me again. That makes me smile. While I may have been calling depression "A Harvester of Souls" in this chapter, there is always another way to look at things, and it doesn't always have to be negative. Depression is a horrible thing that I wouldn't wish upon anyone, but it can teach us so much about life and what we do in that life. So as I've said, if you do know someone who is going through tough times, give them that reassurance they could really use and help them to brighten their future.

Chapter 4
Life's Timeline

If you're like me or know someone like me, you're probably like a lot of people who feel that there are certain things in life that you need to achieve or certain targets to aim for. You may feel that they need to be accomplished at certain times in life or by a certain age. The reasoning behind these particular targets usually comes from particular influences in our lives, family usually being the main ones, but then friends and other people close to your age can also influence these accomplishments. Obviously, these goals will start to play on your mind once you reach the well-known minefield known as adulthood, but even that can be a target that is up for debate.

The targets that I'm talking about are things that you want to do that will allow you to start making a life for yourself. When school starts to near its end is usually when the first major decision will need to be made, that one being, what do I want to do when I leave school? These days there a quite a few options to pick from depending on what career path you want to take. Do you want to go to sixth form? Maybe go to college? Maybe you need a degree for your chosen path and need to go to university. As I said in the previous paragraph, a lot of these decisions can be influenced by our families, and parents are the most common influence. Nowadays with jobs, there tends to be a lot of talk about how it's not what you know, but who you know. This may imply that you want to follow one of your parents into a career that they chose. This was the path that both my older brother Joe and I chose to follow as we both went to the same college to become carpenters. Once we were qualified, we started working for the same company my dad worked for as his apprentice.

Like I said at the start of this chapter, most of these life goals or targets will play on your mind once you reach adulthood and, again, it is an age that will be debated. Is it when you reach a particular age? Most commonly, eighteen or twenty-one. Is it when you do a particular thing like get a job/career or move out into a home of your own? The main reason I've mentioned having parents as the biggest influence on your life choices is because that's what mine were. I based what I needed to achieve or what I should be achieving on the ages that they achieved these particular targets. Thinking about when did they move out? When did they have children? When did they get married?

Once I was in the working world, I started to look towards different influences on life. This went from my parents to my brothers. The biggest reason for this being that we are all from the same generation, as are their wives. My parents had three kids by 1992. My mum was twenty-four, and Dad would have been twenty-seven. They got married in 1996, just after I had turned four. We were living in a ground-floor flat at that particular time. I can't look too much at the times or ages at which they achieved certain things because it was over twenty-five years ago. Times change. Economies change. House prices would have been very different, as would the average price of a wedding or even a weekly food shop. What the problem has been, though, rather than looking at this info this closely, all I could think about was whether I had achieved these goals at these ages.

So like I say, I started to look at my brothers' achievements as they're from my generation. Looking at this day and age and thinking about what I needed to do to be as successful as they are. Joe is married with three sons, has his own home and still works in the carpentry industry. Ben is married with a daughter, has his own home and works as an electrician. Both of their wives were their first serious girlfriends. I think Joe moved out when he was twenty-one, and Ben moved when he was twenty-four. A lot of the time I've been looking at these accomplishments and praying for the day that I will achieve them.

I think that once we start reaching adulthood or once we get ourselves into a job or career, we look at similar goals to these and think that they have to be reached by a certain age or time in the timeline of life. A lot of people will think that if you haven't got onto the property ladder before you're thirty, maybe even twenty-five, that you're a failure… yet I've never had that accusation. Sometimes we think if they don't happen by the age that others got it, and then it might never happen. We start to put pressure on ourselves to try to get ourselves closer to the targets we've set. That pressure starts to feel much heavier once we start looking at friends, people we were at school with or just people we know who are younger than us that are achieving these goals. I know so many people who I went to school with who are now married with kids, have their own home and are even ticking things off their bucket list.

Whether it's what our parents, siblings or friends have achieved, it doesn't necessarily mean that we have to pick the same path they've chosen or do things in the same way they have. We don't need to start putting more stress onto our life; life is very stressful at the best of times. There's no particular structure or method that everyone has to follow in life, and this is one of the reasons that makes it so special. There are no judges that you're trying to impress. A house and a happy family before twenty-one, doesn't get you a special prize. Unless you're an only child, other than your siblings, there'll be no one else who had the upbringing you have had. They might have had a similar one but not the same. This could have changed things a lot for you in life.

We don't all need to live our lives in the same way as everybody else. To be honest, I've probably tried to live my life as different as possible to everyone else I know. First things first, I mentioned that since primary school, I've been known by the nickname of Squidy; it is what I use on my Facebook profile. Most people probably would have preferred going back to their original name, but I like being unique; haven't we got enough Toms in this world?

I remember switching primary schools in 2001 when I was nine years old, everyone was listening to pop music whilst I was listening to Slipknot and getting into metal music. Whilst most people I knew in secondary school went to sixth form then university, I went to college and got myself a trade even though I had the grades that would have allowed me to go to university. After seven years in the building trade, I then realised what I wanted to do in my life as a career. I turned a hobby into a career and became a personal trainer even though, to begin with, I was making more money in the building trade. A lot of people in this situation would have stayed at their original job because they were on a higher wage or didn't want to leave the job or colleagues that they knew, but I took that risk and did what I wanted to make me happy.

With all this in mind, just because a life cycle may be different, just remember that different doesn't always mean bad or worse. I may not have gotten onto the property ladder yet, but a lot of people I know that have gotten on it have had a helping hand from their families. A lot of those who have are also a couple with a joint income rather than doing it by themselves. I may have to work harder to get a place of my own, but just because I haven't done it at the average age of most others doesn't mean it's never going to happen.

If you were to ask me when I was eighteen what I'd be doing when I was twenty-eight, chances are I'd probably have said I'd be a more experienced carpenter. I'd never have thought I would have become a personal trainer or even thought I would be writing this book. We can't accurately predict the future of our lives, but we can decide which paths to take on our journey. We have the power to either decide to stay in a job we hate and live for the weekends because it's better paid, or we can stop and think about what type of career we would rather be doing and what we have to do to get there. I've known so many people who are stuck in a job they hate because if they left then they'd never get to see their work friends again, but then when you ask if they do anything outside of work, the answer's always no. If you were really friends, then you would do things outside of work; a friend only in the workplace is just a colleague.

Another reason we sometimes haven't achieved the things that we want to achieve is because we're often too quick to give up. If we're saving up for something important, we might have a big bill come along or an event that we know will cost a lot, such as a birthday or night out. But rather than decline the invite or stay sober to continue saving, we lose our willpower and then keep repeating these actions and saving up slowly fades from our minds. We're too afraid of letting others down, but I'm sure if you explain to a friend that you can't go because you're saving for a new car or a house, then they'll understand.

Sometimes we often fear that what it is we're trying to achieve will take too long or the work will be too hard. Nothing worth having comes easy. I've listened to a lot of motivational speakers when I've been going through difficult times; one of my favourites is Eric Thomas. One story in particular he tells is of a guy who wants to be successful in business, so he meets up with a business guru who says to meet him at the beach. The guy turns up in a suit but should have brought trunks as the guru tells him to walk out into the sea. Eventually, he gets to head height, and the guru holds him under the water. The guy eventually comes up after doing all he can to get some air. The moral of the story is, if you wish to achieve success as much as you want to live and do all you can to can to get it like you would in trying to survive, then you'll one day achieve that triumph.

This is a quote that I've used a lot and said to a lot of people to try to help them when they're having their own troubles. It's telling you that no matter how long something takes or how difficult it may become, keep on pushing for it. There were a number of times in my teens when I'd be playing a video game and quit because I kept getting frustrated at the number of times I kept dying or couldn't do the level. But I kept playing it. Whether it took all day or the rest of the week, I'd keep coming back to it until I completed it. When I was a personal trainer, I had a fair number of clients who were doing very well for themselves: detached house, multiple cars, and frequent holidays. They might have been in managerial positions at work, but more often than not, they'd be coming home at eight p.m., working the weekends or looking shattered all the time. Yes, they've earned more than most of us, but they have to work their arse off to get it.

One client in particular I remember was in her early thirties and a director of a 3-D printing company. I would say, "I've got a client in Lichfield on Monday, then one in Tamworth Tuesday." She would do this as well, but Monday would be Germany, Tuesday would be Sweden, and her whole week would be spent all over Europe. She had a lovely detached house, a great looking Mercedes SUV, took holidays in Barbados, but even though she was a lovely lady, she looked like a zombie half the time. This just proves that you can achieve the goals you're after, but you have got to be willing to put the time in and make the sacrifices required to get them.

I've already mentioned that I have this particular fear myself, but I think another major issue that makes us give up too easily is the fear of failing. We may do all the hard work we need to do to be where we want to be, but if somebody says no or tells us we're not good enough, we often quit there and then. When going to a job interview or putting in an offer for a house, we need to remember that the response of the other person, more often than not, is just down to one person's opinion. In a job interview, one person may say you're not what they're looking for, but another company may think you fit the bill perfectly.

The offer you put in for a house might not meet the price that person was looking for, but someone with a similar house may think that's spot on or even much more than expected.

We need to remember that famous people or big-brand companies didn't become the success they are today on their first attempt. Colonel Harland David Sanders, a.k.a. Colonel Sanders, who set up KFC, didn't franchise his secret recipe until 1952, when he was sixty-two years old. Leonardo DiCaprio received four Academy Award nominations before finally winning his first Academy Award after his fifth nomination for his role in *The Revenant*. Can you imagine if he had given an interview announcing his retirement from acting because he didn't win when he got his first nomination? In July 1994, an online marketplace for books was founded. Today it is the second-largest private employer in the United States and one of the most valuable companies in the world after reportedly making $232.89 billion in annual revenue in 2018.

Some of you may have guessed, but this company is Amazon. It went from a simple online bookshop to being one of the most valuable companies the world has ever known. It may not have happened overnight, but it just goes to show that if you're willing to put the time and effort in, who knows what you might achieve. Colonel Sanders didn't have a restaurant until he was in his sixties; a lot of people would think you wouldn't have a chance of having a successful business once you pass your fifties or even your forties. Even though it probably sounds corny, one thing Mr DiCaprio has taught us all is if at first you don't succeed, try, try again.

The point of all three of these examples is that it has taken them time and effort to get to where they wanted to be. The colonel has shown us that you can achieve anything you want at any age and that there isn't a particular timeline you have to follow. Leonardo DiCaprio has shown that just because things don't go right for you the first time doesn't mean they'll never go right for you. And with Amazon, they've shown us all that you can never predict what the future will hold for you, but it doesn't have to be from the same path because that's where you started from.

It's like I quoted from Eric Thomas, "If you want to succeed as bad as you want to breathe, then you will be successful." You just have to make sure that you know what it is you want and what you're going to have to do to get there. If you don't start looking at these things, then you may get stuck in your mind with a lot of "what ifs" and be constantly overthinking everything. I'm very sorry to say that it's overthinking a lot of issues that got me into the depressed state of mind that I know. It tends to cause a lot more problems than it solves, often causing problems that you didn't even know were there. The overthinking world can be a horrible and lonely one, so it is very important to keep our minds occupied and motivated. We will achieve the things we want in our lives when we decide, not when others achieve them or when they dictate that we should. We all have what it takes to achieve what we want in our lives; we just have to stop telling ourselves that we don't and believe in ourselves.

Chapter 5
Overthinking: The Well of the Damned

When it comes to depression or anxiety, like anything, there has to be a reason or a cause for it. Quite often, it's because of worries or fears that we have about a particular subject or maybe an event that we have coming up. Unfortunately for us, though, these worries and fears can be caused by ourselves. We start to let our imaginations run wild and think of all sorts of different outcomes and possibilities that could happen, none of which will be positive. Welcome to the deep, dark world of overthinking.

Overthinking is when we don't necessarily know the outcome of something, and we just start to think about every possibility that could happen, no matter how bad it is or how ridiculous it may sound. More often than not, overthinking is going to cause more problems than it will solve. It's just going to get you more worked up and will make you worry even more about whatever the issue is that you have on your mind. A lot of the time as well, even on the rare occasion that we might think of a positive outcome, we tend to dismiss that outcome straight away because we lack confidence or self-belief. That will usually be the outcome that we see as the most ridiculous as we keep thinking about what else could happen.

We've got to think that any word that has "over" in front of it is going to be negative. "Over" is there because we're getting or doing too much of what we need. Oversleeping is bad because you sleep too much, and it can make you late for important events or work. Overeating is bad because we're having too much food, which can lead to obesity and other health problems. Probably the worst of these is an overdose — too many drugs or too much medication will lead to the ultimate in negativity and lead to death. A lot of people I've known who have had depression or anxiety have told me that they overthink things quite frequently, and I believe that it is a huge reason for causing it.

Obviously, there isn't a cure or a quick fix for it, but there are certain things that cause it or can lead to it happening. First and foremost, I think the most common time for it to happen is when we are alone. As we're not with anyone else, listening to what they're saying or focusing on what it is we're doing with them, we give our minds the opportunity to drift off and start dwelling on any negative thoughts we may have on our minds. Sometimes when we might be watching television, we may relate to a story in the show we're watching and start thinking about how we relate to certain negative stories being told. You very rarely tend to catch yourself overthinking something if you're with people or doing something that needs your focus, or attention. I may have said your mind can drift whilst watching television, but in certain activities like work, exercise or even reading, they're all activities that need our mind to focus on the task at hand a bit more than watching television will.

Overthinking is another form of stress, something that I feel quite often is taken for granted. Sometimes people may think, *oh, it'll be fine tomorrow*, or *I'll get over it*. While it's good to have a positive outlook, stress can also lead to health problems. Obviously, there are lots of emotional effects we get from stress, but there are quite a lot of physical effects as well. It can make us feel unwell, cause us to have headaches and also make us have trouble sleeping which can cause lots of problems itself. It can also lead us to use things in excess, such as drugs or alcohol.

Many times in my adult life, I have found that I've had trouble sleeping because of overthinking. It is one of the worst times that you can do it. Like I mentioned before, we tend to overthink when we are alone. I've had relationships but spent most of my adult life as a single man, which gives me even more chance to overthink. But even if you're in a relationship or even happily married, chances are if you're overthinking, your partner is probably asleep, and that's probably one of the reasons you are overthinking at that moment — because you're alone with your thoughts.

Normally when we try to get to sleep, we might be thinking about something, and we'll slowly drift into other thoughts and topics, but we're not really focused on one thing in particular, which is why we eventually drift off. If there is something in particular that we're overthinking, it's usually something bad, and we keep our focus on it and keep thinking about what could happen if the issue isn't solved. For example, if you've got a massive bill coming up but you know you won't be able to pay it, you start to think about what's going to happen if it's not paid. These thoughts also tend to get progressively worse. *Will I get any extra time? Are they going to warn me? Will I incur any penalties? Will bailiffs come round?*

We may have all kinds of thoughts going round our heads and lots of them when we try to get to sleep, but the difference with the thoughts as we overthink is that these aren't just thoughts — they are worries. They make us anxious and make us panic, which keeps us awake. Another problem is, and one that I've suffered from a lot, that as these worrying thoughts keep us up longer and longer, we keep looking at the clock. As we look at the clock, we realise that we will get less and less sleep, which will probably make us feel worse. At that point, you start to *try* to get to sleep, try to force it to happen a bit more. The issue with this is, even though it might sound a bit cheesy, sleep is a bit like love: the more you try to force it, the less chance that it will happen.

So one major problem that overthinking can cause for us is to get less sleep and give us poor sleeping patterns. I feel that sleep in the world of today is a much-underrated commodity. A lot of people think the average person needs seven hours of sleep when actually it's closer to nine hours. When I was working as a personal trainer, I used to tell clients about it all the time and really try to drive home how necessary it is to the human body. When we're sleeping, our body replenishes every type of cell that the body has. That includes muscle cells so that the body can recover from the exercise that it does. Brain cells so that the next morning your brain and mind can function better, and you can function more academically. Your hormones can also be affected, and sleep will help them function more efficiently. This means that sleep deprivation can affect the hormones that regulate things like hunger and appetite in a negative fashion. This was quite often a reason why several of my clients had struggled with losing weight before seeking out a trainer, as they thought weight loss was all down to exercise and nutrition.

In the introduction to this book, I spoke about how I couldn't really understand how people could suffer from anxiety or depression until I began to suffer with it myself. Another example of issues like this that I couldn't understand until I went through them myself was the issues of addiction, mainly alcohol and occasionally drugs. I never saw how people could get so dependent on it. We all have food that we love, like chocolate, but I always thought that alcohol — it's not really a great tasting thing — how could you want so much of it all the time? My only other thought, because my favourite type of music is heavy metal, was that most rock stars drink and do drugs and do it so much so that they can party all the time.

This was sort of the reason that I found with it. As I started working, I started going out at the weekends more and more. It was just the thing you did. You've been working all week for "the Man", and the weekend is ours to do whatever we want and have a blast. But as I got older and discovered that I was suffering with depression, I finally saw how alcohol could seriously affect the lives of others. I never drink alone or just for the sake of it; I've always needed an event or a group of people to be with. Plus, in recent years, my friends and I have started to drink much less. We still socialise, but alcohol doesn't have to be a necessity with socialising.

I remember one night in particular; it was a friend of mines birthday in December 2019, and we were having a surprise costume party at a village hall. This wasn't long after I had lost my last job for medical reasons, and I had a fresh scab on my cheek from having had a seizure face down on a carpet and getting carpet burn. There were lots of people there and lots that I hadn't seen for a while. We had a good catch-up, but the problem was that most of the questions I got were "What are you doing now?" or "What happened to your face?" I didn't want to make up any stories because they always sound ridiculous or unbelievable, so I just told them about my car accident and the seizures I'd been having. Mentioning these issues kept them on my mind, and I found myself drinking quicker than usual. The reason I was drinking faster than normal was to try to get drunk quicker and keep myself happy. It was after this that I realised how alcohol can affect people and why they overindulge.

I also found myself mixing drinks. Rather than just drinking the cans of lager I had taken to the party, I was having shots and the odd Jack and coke that people had offered. There were also a lot of people that I either didn't know or wasn't as good a friend with as others were, so, sometimes, I found myself standing quietly on the outside of the conversation. If you're not talking or involved, you're quietly standing whilst continually taking sips of your drink.

In the end, I was a complete mess. I didn't embarrass myself at the party, but once everyone had left, the worst started to happen. I was supposed to go back to my girlfriend's house that night as she'd gone out with her friends, but for some reason, I didn't get the taxi. They called me telling me what street they were on, but I just kept wandering up and down the street of the village hall. I had a bag of things with me to take to my girlfriend's but found I lost a lot of them. I eventually got a taxi by a main road, about a mile from the party. It only felt like ten to fifteen minutes after the party had ended, but in the end, once I was home, I realised that it had been over two hours. I had called the taxi firm and my girlfriend several times too. From the bag I had taken to the party, I had lost a hoodie, an insulin pen, a walking stick that was part of my costume and my car and house keys. I felt so awful and ashamed of myself beyond belief after talking to my girlfriend the next day.

As I hadn't been able to be officially employed due to my medical issues, I had been doing some gardening work for a friend's mum, to help make a bit of money on the side. She would pick me up as I wasn't allowed to drive, but that week she had to drop some things off at a friend's house. This friend lived in the same village that the party was at. As we drove to her house, I realised that I hadn't just walked up and down the street of the village hall; I had literally walked around every inch of the village, up and down practically every street. I must have been in and out of consciousness because I had no idea at the time how far I'd actually gone.

The results of this night were a serious wake-up call to me, showing me how people can often spiral out of control and into a world of addiction once they have entered the horrible world of depression. Normally I can drink, get drunk but most importantly, still be in control. Because I had so many thoughts on my mind, I was so down at this particular time and had to sort of mention the reasons I was down to people. And because these thoughts stayed on my mind after telling people about them, I was essentially trying to cheer myself up with alcohol. I was basically trying to force myself to be happy rather than think about the issues that were making me depressed.

I haven't heard from many people personally about their problems with drugs and alcohol, but I feel like a lot of people who have had problems with drugs or alcohol may have similar reasons for overindulging in them. Yet again, there's another word with "over" in front of it, and again, it's not something positive. If you are overindulging to simply try to make yourself happier, it's not going to work and can destroy your life.

I may have only got to this stage where I was drinking for happiness on one particular occasion, and I have got drunk since, but as I have normally and with more responsibility, but it could have been much worse. Unfortunately, this was the beginning of the end for me and the girlfriend I was with at the time. We didn't split for a few weeks after, but things weren't the same at all. Then there was all the wandering around the village. Over and over, I've mentioned the seizures that I've been having. What if I had one whilst I was wandering around at two o'clock in the morning, passed out and then choked on my own vomit, or even worse, passed out in the middle of the road? I would hate to have put my friends and family through the horrific feelings they would experience if something like that had happened. Ironically, now I've even just written a paragraph that is, essentially, overthinking.

I don't hate alcohol or want to try to make you hate it and, as I said, I still drink today, just with the same responsibility as I normally would have when drinking in the past. But the main reason for the story of that night is that often people get so depressed that they drink to make themselves happier. The even bigger point is that the main reason I had become so depressed was due to the amount of overthinking that I would do. I had been overthinking about things months and months before this party had even happened, but it was becoming more frequent. Basically, I just want to show you how dangerous overthinking can become.

In my mind, overthinking is the biggest cause for people becoming depressed or starting to suffer with anxiety. Sometimes it can be mistaken as just a phase, but while the issues may not last and can change, you may still overthink certain things. But I also believe that this doesn't mean you have to be stuck with it; there are definitely ways that you can beat overthinking. Like a lot of issues in this book, I think that the best way is to realise and come to terms with the fact that you may be depressed or suffering with anxiety. Though not as easy as it sounds, once you begin doing so, you can start to find out what the causes are for this, and you may find that the problems that you are going through may be down to overthinking.

Chapter 6
Changing Your Focus

So like I said in the previous chapter, I believe that overthinking is one of the biggest reasons people suffer from anxiety and go into depression. If overthinking is when we look into something and think about it too much, surely this must mean that to stop this habit, we need to change our focus and stop worrying so much about the negative thoughts that we have. We must try to keep our minds occupied so that they don't get the chance to drift off into negativity and make us worry more and more about the worrying possibilities that could take place.

I remember when I was going to my wellbeing matters consultations, I told the doctor I was seeing that I did overthink a lot and that I was worried about several different issues that I had going on. He gave me one of the best yet simplest sounding pieces of advice that I'd ever been given. He told me that if ever I thought about a problem and started to worry, rather than worry and make myself feel worse, I should see if I could solve that problem then and there. For example, if you've forgotten about a payment that needs to be paid, check if you're still within the time limit and, if you can, pay it straight away, rather than putting it off to a later date which will probably make you start panicking again once that date comes around. The problem has been taken care of, and you have one less worry.

Obviously, not all problems can be solved straight away, so if you can't solve it, think about whether or not it is really going to affect you and whether it is something within your control. For example, with this one, say you're going to some kind of social event, and you're trying to impress someone, or you're worried about what people might think about how you look. If the person you are trying to impress is a love interest and nothing really progresses with them, is it the end of the world? Was that the last opportunity you'll ever have? Does it mean you'll never have any chance with anyone ever again? I doubt it. When it comes to what people think of you, there's a very important word in that phrase… that word is *think*. This isn't a proven fact, ninety-nine per cent of people who have a negative opinion of you, will keep it to themselves, it's doubtful they will come face to face with you and say what they're thinking. More often than not, if they do come up to you and say something, chances are it'll be a compliment.

Not everyone will have the same kinds of thoughts or negative feelings about certain things, but these are just example methods offering an alternative to deal with these bad thoughts rather than overthinking and making yourself feel worse. The main point is that if a problem can be sorted and dealt with, then deal with it so it doesn't come back and keep bothering you. Also, the feeling that you get when an issue has been dealt with is so much greater than the mild feeling you get by just thinking, *I'll do it later.*

It shows us that we need to take action if we are to better ourselves and come out of the holes that we are in. I know I may sound like I'm repeating myself with this, but overthinking is exactly what it says on the tin, and that is thinking too much. Unless we're thinking of how to beat an issue, just thinking about it isn't going to make us feel any better. If we keep feeling down, then we're never going to pick ourselves up. Don't get me wrong; it's OK not to be OK. Honestly, I've had my share of tears as an adult, and quite often, getting it out can be a good release. But if we just keep feeling sorry for ourselves all the time, how are we ever going to be happy again? The right people will help you in your life, but if you're always mopey or always looking for pity, even when they're doing their best to help you, they will get tired of it and eventually move on.

One of the most common instances where I have seen people not taking action, and you have probably seen a few examples of it yourself, is when people are not happy with their jobs or careers. Quite regularly, you will see people who hate their job and are pretty open about it, but it doesn't get them down, and they carry on. But then there are other people on the other side of the coin, and they are the type who will constantly moan about how bad their job is and how they would love to do something else. More often than not though, when you give these people some ideas about further education or looking into another career, the reason they don't want to try something new is because they might not see a particular colleague again, or the work they'll have to do will be too hard.

If a work friend is a real friend, then you will see them outside of work. You will never know unless you try, and unless you try the work you will need to do to get yourself a new career, how will you know if it will be difficult or not? I can understand that we all suffer from low self-esteem or confidence from time to time, but if you look back to the moral of the Eric Thomas story in chapter four — when you want success as much as you want to breathe, you will succeed — what that is essentially saying is that if things are as bad as you think they are right now, then you will do anything you have to do to make them better, no matter how difficult it is.

If there are more issues than just getting new qualifications, look into what it is you'll have to do to solve those. When I wanted to learn how to become a personal trainer, I couldn't get time off work to go to college, so I found a company that would allow me to do my learning from home. I couldn't afford to pay for the training course in one payment, so when looking for a company, I made sure to find one that would let me pay for it on a monthly basis. Anything in life that is worth having won't come easy, and we have to take action to make progress.

Sometimes we continue to do things that we hate or upset us simply for financial gain. I've seen people in similar situations to the ones I have just mentioned where they hate the job that they're in but simply don't want to leave because the pay is good, and they don't think they'll get a better or manageable wage elsewhere. Probably one of the most common and important lessons that we'll learn in life is that money doesn't always lead to happiness. Though it may ease any financial pressures we have and pay for things that we enjoy, it doesn't guarantee happiness.

I've spoken about some of the clients that I had as a personal trainer, and they are a perfect example of what I mean when I say money doesn't always mean happiness. One couple I remember working with seemed to be raking it in. They had a huge detached five-bedroomed house, both had brand new Range Rovers, and their two boys both went to private school. But because I trained them individually, you could see their behaviour and feelings towards each other a bit more clearly, and they did often moan about each other. It wasn't all the time but, unfortunately, it was more often than not. Just goes to show that money can't buy you everything.

But going back to careers, even though they may pay you well, it doesn't exactly mean that you're certain to enjoy it. Great pay doesn't always mean a great job.

If people find themselves in this position, they tend not to want to go to a job that will pay less, even if it's a job that they absolutely adore or will continue to help them get by, just with fewer luxuries.

The point I'm trying to highlight here is that if we want to make our lives better and lead a happier life, we need to take action. We have to do things to help improve our situation. If you are just going to continue to be upset and think about how bad things can get, it isn't going to get you anywhere or help you push forward. As I have spoken about many times before already, overthinking can make us upset, and it usually happens when we're alone or idle. If we've solved the problems that we can solve but there are still things on our mind, then we need to occupy ourselves with something that can take our mind off them and get us to be more positive.

One of the best things that can help us with this can be to exercise more. Now you may think that I'm just saying this as a former personal trainer, but exercise can help us physically and mentally. When we exercise, the body releases chemicals known as endorphins. These interact with receptors that are found in the brain and reduce your perception of pain. They also trigger positive feelings similar to the effect found with morphine. Exercise can help relieve stress, and if done regularly, it can help improve your self-esteem. As well as mental health, exercise can improve your sleep, strengthen your heart, lower blood pressure, reduce body fat and obviously improve your overall fitness and health.

My favourite type of exercise is strength and resistance training. It's something that I've done for a number of years. It's brilliant for my self-esteem because it helps me feel better when I increase the reps that I'm doing or the weight of the weights that I'm lifting. This shows me what I'm capable of and shows me the improvements that I am making in my training; this makes me feel good. Because I'm counting the number of repetitions and sets I'm doing, it keeps my focus on the exercises rather than making me think about any stressful issues that I may have on my mind.

There are many types of exercise that you can do these days. It doesn't necessarily have to be just signing up to a gym and using a treadmill or bike for an hour. Look into all the different sorts of clubs or classes that are available in your area. Maybe look into learning something while you exercise like a martial art. It doesn't even have to be something sport-related — look into taking up dancing — pole aerobics and fitness is especially popular nowadays. If your anxiety is particularly bad or you're just not a people-person, with how much the world of technology and the internet has developed, you can find all sorts of instructional videos that could help you with these types of skills and exercises online. Even if you choose to follow one type of exercise, they have a massive range of variations and different levels. Yoga is a perfect example of this as you have some yoga styles that focus on general fitness, some more focusing on the spiritual side of things and even some that simply focus on relaxation with different breathing techniques.

As great as exercise can be, it's not the only thing that can help to change our focus. There is a whole range of topics and hobbies that we can look into that can help to keep our minds occupied so that we don't find ourselves falling into the dreaded world of overthinking. This can vary from small activities such as puzzles or reading books to even looking into new activities you've never done before, such as archery or indoor rock climbing. You can look online for all kinds of activities and find your local clubs or facilities.

More often than not, the more creative a hobby or topic is, the better it will be for keeping our minds busy. Things such as gardening are brilliant examples but, obviously, these can't take place all year round due to autumn and winter. But things such as crafts are very popular these days; even my mum and sisters-in-law attend a weekly craft club that's local to us. It covers a whole range of different activities such as arts and crafts, knitting and sewing and even things like model making. It doesn't necessarily have to be one of these activities; as previously mentioned, if we look online, we're sure to find all sorts of different hobbies we could start doing from a number of different areas. Just remember, though, one point I raised earlier is that you don't have to do these particular activities. Find something you enjoy, find your own way. My suggestions can help, but that doesn't mean it's the only way; five plus five equals ten, but so does six plus four.

The issue that I'm raising here is that we don't have to be trapped in our heads or be swallowed by the troubles that we have going on in our lives. I can also appreciate that there will be troubles that aren't as simple to get over by just trying to change our focus with a new hobby. However, what I'm trying to say at this point is that if we have issues that concern overthinking and they cause us to feel upset most of the time, then doing nothing to try to change these issues means that nothing is going to happen.

If we moan about being hungry but then don't eat, we will still be hungry. If we want a happier or better life, then we have to make something happen. An opportunity isn't just going to fall into your lap. There are rare occasions when you hear a story of a famous model just suddenly being discovered whilst they were out and about, but I bet they took steps to eat healthily, exercise and look after their body. Though they didn't go to a modelling agency to get the job, they took the actions necessary to look like a model so that a rare chance of being discovered was there.

Again though, we can't all just depend on a chance like this happening to us. We have to get out there and take action in our lives to progress. If you can't get over the horrible feelings that you have, then always remember, chances are there is someone somewhere in a much worse position. If you're not dying and there is a roof over your head, are the concerns you have really worth worrying so much about? Like I wrote earlier, sometimes people worry about things they've never done; if you've never done it, then why does that immediately mean it's going to be negative?

When I left school, I had never been on a building site before; I had never been a carpenter before. Yet, after years of doing it, I may not have enjoyed it, but the point is, I was able to do it and become a successful carpenter. I didn't know anyone in my class at college, but, in time, I started to get on with them and made friends. I'm sure you've had situations like this in workplaces and at other times in your life. This just shows that we do have the power to take action in our lives and make them better. An example of this is writing this book. I've never written before, and I don't know if it will get published, but if I don't give it a go, then I will never find out.

We can all lose confidence in ourselves and lose the motivation we need to drive us forward or push us on. Nevertheless, I can guarantee there were times you had done this before depression or anxiety. There were positive thoughts in at least one stage of your life. We weren't born depressed. It's not simple or straightforward, but this shows that we've believed in ourselves and have been happy before, and we can find the strength we need to get back to those feelings in our lives. We can change our focus, and we can make this situation that we're in a whole lot better, as long as we can take hold and take action.

Chapter 7
The Release

Before we continue, please note that in this chapter, reader discretion is advised as there are some dark issues raised.

In my opinion, it doesn't matter how tough you are, how rich or successful you may be or if you have it all in life, I think that everyone at some point in their life will feel some kind of mental or emotional anguish. These can be a whole range of different emotions or feelings. These can include pain, anger, hate, jealousy, envy, sorrow and more. I know that in my adult life, I have felt most of these at some stage, and these have led to the depression that I have experienced.

What started it for me was feeling a lot of hatred and anger towards people. I've felt a lot of anger towards people who treated me or others like less or even looked down on us. This has led to me feeling pretty horrific levels of hatred towards these people too. Many of these people included bosses and managers who I had worked for in the building trade. Many of them thought they were better or more important than others and walked around the sites with an arrogant swagger.

Like a lot of people, we may have ill feelings towards people that we meet for a whole range of different reasons. Sometimes there can be people that we don't have a particular reason for not liking other than that they are just annoying or irritating. Other times there is a more specific reason. I remember in my early twenties, there was a particular girl that I fancied and had been chasing for a number of years. There had also been a number of other guys doing the same who knew I liked her, and they would be very passive-aggressive or sarcastic towards me if we all met up to go out with other friends. Eventually, though, I would learn that the girl I was chasing was just using me. She knew how much I liked her and that I'd do anything for her. She used this to her advantage, and it sickened me — how someone had the nerve to do that to somebody and take it so far.

I've said that I overthink things quite a lot and have had trouble sleeping in the past because of it. There have also been times where these thoughts have become quite dark and disturbing as well. Often when trying to sleep, I try to imagine particular things to try to make my mind drift off and hopefully allow me to fall asleep. With these people that I have mentioned who I have hated or felt considerable anger towards, I often try to realise these feelings in these dark thoughts. It may seem terrible and awful, but I have often despised them so much that I have pictured scenes of me torturing them. These are often quite graphic thoughts that can match the level of horror films and even serial killers. Usually, it's because the people I'm picturing are the bosses and managers that I've worked for in the past because I can't let my feelings out towards them for the obvious risk of being fired. I feel like they are so despicable and have no sense of heart or goodness within them that they need to be punished. It may seem hypocritical of me to say that they're not good after I've described torturing them, but they have no sense of decency and only care for themselves. I know this isn't the best thing to mention, but I'm just being open and honest; I can only apologise if I have offended anybody.

As you have already read, the biggest feeling of mental anguish that I have experienced is being jealous or envious of others who I feel have had more available to them or maybe haven't had to work as hard for the things that they have in life. I can't help it if people have been born into more successful or richer families, but in these times of social media, when I see people who constantly post pictures of what they have as if they're showing off and just looking for more likes... it just makes me feel like more of a failure and makes me doubt myself more that I'll ever make it in life. More often than not, it's the materialistic people who do this that bug me the most.

Nowadays, it has almost turned into a culture, more often than not coming from reality TV stars who get onto one show with no skills or talent and are then offered appearances on other shows because of the number of people they have following them on Twitter or Facebook — people they've never met and have had no input in their lives whatsoever. Yet, for some reason, this is the celebrity culture of today and, unfortunately, this is what so many people of today want to be like, look like and act like. Then yet again, when I see their so-called "success" and materialism, these jealous and envious feelings turn back into anger and hatred.

Unsurprisingly, it's these reality stars I then have horrific images of. Hurting them, injuring them, in my mind giving them something they deserve, something they have well and truly earned. I don't have anything against these people personally. They were given an opportunity, and they took it. The feelings that I feel towards them are ones that I believe are quite common in this day and age. This isn't to say that everyone has homicidal thoughts towards people they despise, but I think that there are many out there who think that some people have been very undeserving of the riches and successes that they have. They feel like they have had to work so hard to get to where they are and still not be where they should be, whereas others have met minimal requirements to get to their luxurious styles of living.

It's these feelings and more that have led to me feeling the sadness that I have felt. It's not anyone's fault; sometimes we can't help the way that we feel. With depression and anxiety, you often go through things that you hear a lot about when it comes to these feelings of anguish. I have, on occasion, fallen out of love with things that I normally would enjoy. My fitness has dropped, which has led to me putting on some weight and falling out of shape. People do tell you that you're not the same person they used to know. While we can get help, we don't lose these negative feelings to a point where we'll never feel them again and forever be happy. But we can do things that will give us a release from these emotions, and they can be managed. We all, at some point, will need some kind of release from our lives.

Even if we don't deal with the issues of anxiety or depression, we still need a release from a whole range of issues in our lives. Everyone needs a break from their careers from time to time; this is why we have holidays. You love your family, but even they can sometimes get too much, and this is why we have babysitters in the world. Whatever the feeling or emotion may be, we have to be able to release it. If we hold things in or dwell on problems for too long or continuously, they won't get better and will eventually erupt at the worst of times. As I talked about in the chapter "Changing Your Focus", there is a whole range of things that can help us let go of any ill feelings that we may be keeping inside ourselves.

For me, one of the biggest releases is being different. Though I may not be as successful as others, I like to be my own person and to be an individual. So as I said to you already, most people know me as Squidy. I could just carry on as Tom, but I feel like I'm standing out and being my own person as Squidy. I also don't like to follow trends or fads. I don't listen to pop music or what's in the charts; I don't follow fashions or try to match celebrities. I like to be my own person and live my own life. This makes me feel positive because it makes me feel that I have self-respect and that I don't need to try to change who I am to impress or fit in with other people. Always be you, and if people don't like it, then that's tough for them, and they will just have to live with it.

I know I spoke about it a lot in the previous chapter, but creative outlets can be a massive release for any emotional or negative feelings that we may come across in our lives. One big outlet that I'm sure many of you have felt gives you a release is music. Depending on the type of music or song, they can make us feel all types of different states of mind after hearing them. Sad songs can make us cry and make us let out some tears whereas happy or joyful songs can make us feel all kinds of different emotions. These can include happiness, pride, inspiration and can even make us feel silly. My favourite genre of music is heavy metal. This can help me release aggression and energy and can even motivate me when I need it to get me to want to do some of my weight training.

Several times it has allowed me to release some energy and aggression. As well as listening to music, I also play bass guitar. I often play along to the songs I enjoy, and while doing so, I will be head banging or dancing around the room. Another example of this is when I have been to gigs or music festivals. Seeing live bands is such an amazing thrill. Head banging and going into the mosh pits — it's such an energetic release. While doing all of these musical-related activities, at no point will my mind start thinking about any problems or issues I need to resolve. I'm sure after a break-up we've all listened to a sad song, but those just make us miss or think about whoever the person was. But all of these other activities I've talked about have been a great way to release any frustration or negativity that I have going on. Music has played a huge part in my mental health; it has helped me so much, and it will continue to do so.

It's something that I have talked about already, but if we need a mental release, doing something physical is a perfect way to do so. Probably the emotion I've described the most is anger, and this, sometimes, if bottled up, can lead to some forms of destructive behaviour. This could be just breaking things out of rage, or worse, it could lead to hitting someone or getting into confrontations and fights. Again, this is another time where, for me, getting into my weight training is ideal. I've got the motivation; the energy I have is only being put into one thing, and by the end of it, I'll be too tired to express any rage I have, but, more importantly, I will have forgotten why I was angry in the first place.

With a lot of sports and exercise, your focus and concentration are key attributes to your success in these activities, and you'll no longer be focusing on any negatives you have going on at that time. Sporting activities especially are very competitive, so any aggression that you may have bottled up can be converted into desire or a competitive edge.

I've brought up how people can get jealous of others. For me, it's being jealous of what others have or their level of success, but sometimes we feel that having what the people we are jealous of have will get rid of those feelings altogether. Though I haven't got there yet, I believe that this isn't always going to be the case. We can often think that if we won the lottery, for example, that all of our problems would be solved, and we'd never be unhappy ever again. It is probably one of the most talked about issues you could think of and also has a very popular saying which is, "Money can't buy you happiness." Don't get me wrong, lots of it is going to make you happy, but that doesn't necessarily mean you'll never have any negative feelings ever again.

Not long ago, I remember watching Cristiano Ronaldo on a television programme where he had an hour-long interview with Piers Morgan. This was more about his life, his upbringing and his family rather than his football career. A lot was revealed in this interview, including the fact that Ronaldo is worth an estimated $500 million. He has around seventeen supercars, houses all over Europe; there's very little he can't buy. But in one section of the interview, he spoke about his children and how they stay on the grounds of the house more often than not. This is because, as much as he wants to, if Ronaldo went to the park with his children, he wouldn't be able to spend time with them as he would be mobbed by fans who would all want pictures and autographs.

I remember seeing such a sad expression on his face when he said this to Piers. He has four children, all under ten; just imagine hundreds of strangers rushing up to your father in huge crowds like that; it would be terrifying. This coming from a man who is worth half a billion dollars. Who is one of the greatest, if not *the* greatest footballer there has ever been. A man who has played for the best teams and won all the trophies he could possibly win at those clubs. Yet even with all of this, more than anything, he'd just like to create some memories with his children. If that doesn't show you that money doesn't buy you everything, then I don't think that anything will.

He may not have said it in the most direct fashion, but I agree with Ronaldo, and I think that one of the best ways to get a release from any negativity that you're currently feeling or going through is to socialise. Whether it's with your family or friends, these are the people that not only know you the best, but most importantly, they care about you the most. To me, friends will have a slight edge on family because you can talk to them about anything. Sometimes there are subjects that you don't want your family to hear, or you don't feel comfortable talking to them about. With friends, however, it doesn't matter how stupid or embarrassing it may be, a true friend's feelings towards you will never change. This will be a massive help if there's ever something you need to let go of.

Though socialising is one of the best releases, I feel that it is a key tool for what I think is the best of all releases out there. Unfortunately, though, it is also probably the hardest way to release something as well. When it comes to our mental health, a lot of the ways to help are a lot easier said than done. The best way to get a release is to talk about it. To actually let go of it, stop keeping it a secret and talk about how you are feeling and how it has been making you feel.

If you keep it inside, all you are going to do is keep thinking about it, dwelling on it and making things worse. A scab that is continuously picked will never heal. Like in previous chapters, if you have a negative mindset, we'll never feel positive. However, if we speak to someone, someone we know and trust and talk about our current situation, chances are that they will have a different outlook. They will help you try to see a more positive side to what's going on rather than being stuck in this harmful spiral that you are in. Getting it out will literally allow you to let go and release any pressure you are feeling, and this can be a major step to help you to improve whatever it is that affects you.

There is nothing wrong with having feelings of negativity in your life; it's OK not to be OK. Sometimes even those who seem to have it all and are on top of the world sometimes need a break from it all as well. Just remember that if we keep hold of our negativity and bottle it up, then it will never improve. Make sure you get the breaks you need and get involved in the things that will help you get that release.

Chapter 8
Strengthen Before Collapse

Throughout this book, I have talked about things that are a lot easier said than done; sorry to say, but yet again, we come to another one of those situations. In this chapter, I want to talk about helping other people rather than just looking at our own circumstances. The title of this chapter is "Strengthen before Collapse", and what I mean by this is that we should try to help those close to us with any bad issues that they might be going through before there's a chance of those issues getting as dark as some of the feelings we may have felt.

I think that in the times that we live in, a lot of people just expect things to happen. A lot of people think that if they go through difficult times, then lots of people will come through for them and help them out. I don't think there are enough people out there who treat people how they want to be treated, and they just expect that they'll receive certain things if ever a time arises when they need that thing. I don't want to call people selfish, but I believe that in today's world, there is too much focus on ourselves, and the only time we think about others is usually when we're worrying about what they think about us or how they will judge us.

Basically, what I want to get across is that I think we should look out for others and do it a lot more than we already do. At this moment in time, as I write this, we are living through the coronavirus pandemic, and we are in lockdown. There has been a particular advert that has bothered me where a woman has made a video for herself to watch in six months' time. In this, she asks herself how she is and then says, "Because we really mean it at the moment." This has angered me every time I see it.

Do we not mean it on any other occasion? Were we only saying it for the sake of it at any other time that we asked? It's almost as if we have to wait for a bad event to happen or for someone to go through bad times before we ask if they are OK or if they are getting on all right. Like I've previously mentioned, anxiety and depression are at an all-time high right now, and I don't think we should be waiting for people to start going through it before we try to help them out of it. If we can solve a problem before that problem gets bigger, then we should do all we can to do so.

Obviously, this doesn't mean we need to ask everyone and anyone if they're OK, but if you see a friend or family member who isn't quite acting like themselves or is a bit quieter than usual, don't be afraid to ask if they're OK. With people we are close to, more often than not, you will find that they don't want to upset you, so they might just pass it off and say, "Oh yeah, I'm fine." They might act as if everything is OK.

But if you are someone who has been through or is going through some dark feelings of your own, you can remember the things you may have said or done when people have asked you how you were.

I can remember times when I've been out with people in the past, and they asked how I was, and straight away I'd say, "Yeah, things are OK." Then I would just put a positive spin on it all and be stereotypical about certain things, things like how work is an annoyance, but at least it pays the bills. I never want to upset friends or family. I certainly don't want to bring the mood down if I'm out with everyone.

"How are things, Squidy?"

"Well, they're as crap as crap can be. No job, no girlfriend, still living with Mum, so everything is glorious!"

Nobody wants to be a liar, but there are times in life that will just call for it.

With our friends, I feel that if there is any negativity that we are going through, we'll tend to hide it more with them than we might with others. As I've just said, we don't want to upset any of our friends, and when we socialise, these are usually plans that we've made in advance. When we do meet up, chances are that we will act much happier and pretend that things are much better than they actually are. With friends, we'll probably have a laugh and joke around, whereas when we are around family, we might just mope around the house. Another example of this is when people say not to work with family. I know about this, having worked with my brother and dad when I first went into carpentry. Chances are if things go wrong, with family you will be more likely to be angry and lose your cool, whereas if you're working with a friend, you will still probably tell them it's wrong but stay calm and speak in a lower tone or even have a laugh about it.

The point is, though, not everybody wants to talk about any negative feelings that they may have straight away. It's good to check in on people, but that doesn't mean you should ask them every day or keep pressuring them for an answer. You may find that you get a more honest answer a bit later on in the day, maybe a call or a text message. They may say something like, "Hey, when you asked me if everything was OK, well truth is… things aren't as good as I said," or something along those lines. A big reason for this is, as I've spoken about, people will tend to hide behind a mask. We don't want to upset people, and we find it harder to talk about upsetting things to someone's face because when we do this, we see the emotions come out as we speak to them.

This is why when it comes to something like breaking up, a lot of times in television programmes when it happens, it'll be by a letter or a voice mail message. This is also why I mentioned that you might get a message later on because whoever it is you're speaking to doesn't want to upset you. I've posted a couple of videos on my Facebook page where I was basically coming clean with how I had actually been feeling over the past couple of years. Telling everyone what had happened and the things I'd been through in that time and how it was truly making me feel. I did this because I have quite a lot of my family on Facebook as well as friends, and it's easier to explain with something they will all see, rather than to lots of individuals at lots of different times. The main reason I made a video, though, is that it is much easier for me to talk to a phone screen than it is to talk to someone I really care about. While it was still a very emotional experience, it was easier for me to keep myself together rather than if I was explaining things in person to a close friend or family member.

Sometimes when people are going through rough times, it might not be as easy as simply recognising they are not being themselves or just being a bit quieter than usual. This is something that I have experienced myself, and I'm sure there are a lot of other men out there who have felt similar to this as well. That's not to say that women won't have felt like this, but it's just in my experience, I've known guys to do this more often than women. Sometimes pride will often get in the way of their true emotions. When friends are trying to organise a night out or an event, there may be one person in the group who's usually always up for it but on this occasion might say they can't really afford it right now and will have to give it a miss. Like I said, I've done this a few times. If you're lucky like me to have some awesome mates, they will just offer to pay for you, no questions asked. But if it isn't you, and it's someone else in the group, even though they may not want to talk about it, don't be afraid to ask if everything's OK or ask if something has happened financially or even at work.

As I have said throughout this chapter, don't keep pushing it or try to force an answer out of them. I've just said it in the last paragraph, a lot of times, pride might get in the way, or they may feel embarrassed or even ashamed about the situation. I know whenever I've had financial troubles, or I had to ask someone for help with it, I always felt a bit ashamed because it was as if I couldn't get by on my own or I was failing. I've always prided myself on being someone who is very independent and will succeed no matter what issues may come my way. But the fact that you're checking in on them will itself make them feel a bit better as it shows that they will have someone there for them when they need it the most.

There are some other cases where people might be going through the worst of times, but they don't see it themselves. They know that what they are experiencing isn't a positive thing, but they may not think it's as bad as it actually is. Basically, what I'm getting at with this is you may find someone who doesn't show any signs of difficulty whatsoever. They are themselves, as enthusiastic as ever, very talkative, and everything is going as well as it was ten years ago. But then, out of nowhere, they may pull you aside and ask to talk to you. They might put something on social media, similar to what I did, and come clean about things not being as good as people may have thought they were. When things like this do happen, it kind of brings me back to what I was mentioning at the start of this chapter.

It's when a lot of us just expect things to happen. Not expecting things to happen, like posting how bad things are for you at the moment on social media and hoping lots of people comment. It's more the people that do comment. I'm not saying that everyone comments like this — I've even done it myself on occasion — but far too often, when someone posts a negative status or is feeling really down, you'll see the familiar, one-phrase comments of "Here if you need me x" or "Here if you want to talk x".

It's good to let someone know you're there for them, and it's not everyone, but a lot of people I've known in the past and seen do it, it's as if they feel like because I've said this, then that means I've helped them out, and I'm such an amazing person.

If the person who shared didn't need someone to talk to or want someone there for them, then they wouldn't have posted whatever it was that made you comment. Don't just tell them you're available if they need to talk; go and talk to them! Pick up the phone and call or message them directly. Tell them that you've seen what they've said and you want to make sure that they are OK. It will show them that you are a much more caring friend by the fact that you want to know if they are OK and that you've directly asked if there's anything you can do to help rather than being one of many who just leave a comment.

It's a man who I have already spoken about in this book, but on my Instagram page, I posted a quote which is deemed to have come from Heath Ledger, by writer Christen O'Brien.

Christen has written about it, talking about the Heath she knew in an online publication known as *Human Parts*. She claims that that this was basically a poetic way of Heath saying that he was a Hollywood actor.

What it basically suggested to me was that when we meet someone new in our lives, we tend to chat about particular things. We get to know the person and get the ball rolling by asking each other particular questions about our current lives. Where are we from? What do we do for a living? Do we have a partner? But even if we are married, living in a mansion and run a successful business, we never get asked whether this makes us happy.

Since I saw the quote, it has always meant a lot to me and has had a lot of significance in the way I see life. In this age of social media, where everyone will always post a photo of their latest holiday, their new house or new car, sure, I know that they've worked for it and done what they had to get those things, but it is another way to show off as they just want to see how many likes they will get. I know people will disagree, but every photo we post, me included, will be to see how many likes we get. What other reason is there for it?

Like I said earlier, we can feel jealous and envious of what others have and seeing it on social media may cause this, but that doesn't mean that it's their fault or they've caused it. With the quote from Heath, even if you are married, have your own home or a great car... people still won't ask you if you are happy. Like most people, we will just assume that if you have all of these things, then you must be happy and have absolutely no reason not to be. In previous chapters, I talked about how having lots of money and lots of materialistic things doesn't necessarily mean you'll be happy. Plus, if this is the case, sometimes you'll get people who mention someone they know who has gone through worse, but they didn't moan, and they didn't feel sorry for themselves, so you should remember how lucky you really are.

The thing we all need to remember, though, is that we are all built and wired differently. Just because one thing doesn't upset you, doesn't mean it won't upset someone else. Throughout this chapter, I think the main topic has been how people mask their feelings, so if someone you know may have everything you'd want in life, it doesn't mean that there isn't something else going on that is tearing them apart inside. So maybe, if we do find ourselves talking to someone we haven't seen for a while or just chatting to a friend, why not start with, "How's life?" If you talk to somebody about their career, ask them if they enjoy it. Even if it comes up, ask if there's ever anything they might need help with or need to talk about.

I'm hoping that this chapter, "Strengthen Before Collapse," is like Ronseal and does exactly what it says on the tin. If we see somebody struggling or going through a hard time, let's see if we can help out. See if we can build them back up before things get really bad and they do fall on the worst of times. But just remember who it is we're trying to help. Whether it's a friend or a family member, it's *them* that we are trying to help.

In an opening scene of the movie *Fight Club*, two of the main characters are at a support group meeting for people who are terminally ill. They pair up like the rest of the group and talk to each other. Neither of them is actually dying or even ill, so they ask each other why they go to these support groups. The male character says, "When people think you're dying, they really listen to you rather than—"

He is then interrupted by the female character who says, "Just waiting for their turn to talk?"

Quite often, when people have conversations and, believe me, I've done this myself, people will wait until they can have their say and then become the main subject of the conversation. When we want to help people, we need to listen. We don't want to start by telling the person about our troubles because it will just make the other person feel undervalued or unappreciated because you're not willing to hear them out. The main thing is if you step back and listen to what has caused them to feel this way, it allows them to get it all out and get it off their chest. I've mentioned how bottling things up will make them feel worse, so getting it out will ease a lot of pressure and tension. But the fact that you have really listened to what they are saying will show them what a great friend they have in you and that they can really rely on you when needed.

With this, it may also make them remember this particular time that you were listening to them and helping them out in their hour of need. So if ever the shoe is on the other foot, it will make them want to help you out, as you did with them. I'm not saying that you should do things for people just so you can get things from them, but rather than just expecting things to happen or people to just help you when required, if you give a helping hand to those without being called upon, then there may be more people out there who want to help you when you are in need of a helping hand. So with this in mind, always keep an eye on those who are closest to you and don't be afraid to ask if everything is OK. If someone isn't happy, you may be that person who can get them closer to the happiness they are looking for.

Chapter 9
The Right People

Probably one of the earliest lessons you will learn in life, if not the first lesson, is that you can't pick and choose your family. If you are the youngest sibling like I am, they will always be there. If you do have siblings, these are usually the first friends that you will have in life. You'll also know that, like friends, you won't always see eye to eye all the time either. Another very important lesson that I have learnt, though, is that no matter what happened when you were younger, no matter how many times you fought or fell out with each other, your family will always be there for you.

With the subject of this book being depression, the biggest trigger for my feelings of depression is that of the feeling of failure and letting others down... especially those close to me. It's already been said, but my two older brothers have already achieved a lot of the things that I wish to achieve. I'll get there at some point but not achieving it around the age that they did does make me feel like I have disappointed my family. But no matter how close to the edge I get, they always reassure me, never lose faith in me and are always proud of what I have done and what I'm doing in my life.

These feelings are also feelings that are mirrored with friends. I have a lot of friends that have achieved what I wish to achieve, and I sometimes feel embarrassed that I'm not quite on their level yet. But they always help me and reassure me. They often remind me that there are sometimes things that I've achieved that they haven't and that I've helped them with issues that they may have had in the past. One friend I can think of in particular is married, has a son and has a flat, but he still is yet to pass his driving test, which he's dying to do, something I did a long time ago. Friends may not technically or officially be family, but they are just as close as and sometimes closer than the people we have in our family. But the important thing is that the right people in our lives are people that we can trust, people that we can rely on no matter what, and people that will always be there for us without us even having to ask. We may not always pick and choose them, but if you are lucky… you won't even have to.

As we transition from our teenage years into adulthood, we go through a lot of changes, and we learn a lot of lessons. One major lesson is that of friendship. Up to the time that we leave school, most of our friends, if not all of them, have been people that we have met through school, and we feel that we will be friends with them forever. This can be the case with some, but this is also usually the time that we learn that friends will come and go.

I can remember the autumn of 2008. This was the year that I finished secondary school and was heading to college to study carpentry. Most of my friends went on to the sixth form to do their A-Levels and get the grades they needed to get into university. I remember a lot of people telling me that I was capable of getting into university, and I knew this, but the fact of the matter was that I just didn't want to go to university. Like I said earlier in the book, I didn't know straight away what I wanted to do when I left school, but I knew I wanted to work and do something physical, something that involved manual labour. After seeing the kind of money that my brother was earning at the time, I knew getting a trade was the answer for me.

I think the real reason that people were telling me I was capable of getting into university was because they were afraid of us drifting apart and losing our friendship. Believe me, I was just as worried about this as well, and I reassured them that we would meet up after school and college like we normally would, and we did. People would have parties, as we all turned eighteen, we started going out on the town, it was great. As I was only at college twice a week and didn't start working until my second year there, I would often go to the school for the last hour and just walk into the sixth form centre. The teachers recognised me and knew I was only sitting in on free periods, so they didn't really have an issue with it. There was the one time that I walked in, just as dinnertime ended, with a four-inch red

Mohawk, which caused quite a big stir as kids surrounded me as if an alien had just landed, but other than that, the teachers didn't have any problems with me coming in.

As sixth form ended and everyone started heading off to university, it was still as if nothing had changed. With most of my friends who stayed home and, like me, were passing their driving tests, we often went to see different friends at different universities and stay over for the weekend. We'd go up for people's birthdays and go out around whichever town or city they had gone to. It was great because we all liked going out, but it was brilliant to go out somewhere we'd never been before. Especially when we usually only go out in Lichfield, which has severely limited places to go to. Even just the car journeys up there were a great laugh.

Unfortunately, though, because people made new friends at university, our contact started to lessen. After the first year or so, we wouldn't go up as much. A lot of the work I was doing as an apprentice carpenter was to refurbish student accommodation. I'd often get students staring at me, and because I thought it was due to them thinking they were better than me because I was in a high-vis vest and working in construction, I'd give them evil looks. Often when we went to visit mates, I'd usually find one of their new friends that I didn't like because they were so pretentious. It wasn't all of them but there always seemed to be one who seemed to roll their eyes when I told them what I did for a living. They also used to rush into pretending like nothing happened when I questioned them on it.

I may have been losing touch with some friends, as they got closer to people they were at university with, but I was doing the same back at home. I went out with friends I went to school with, and they'd introduce me to some of their other friends, then those would introduce me to their friends, and it snowballed. Now after over ten years since leaving school, practically all of my friends in my closest circle are just like I am and came up in the same way. All of them are from working-class families who have earned and worked for everything they have. This doesn't mean you can only have friends with similar upbringings to you or who have the same likes and hobbies, though.

For years as a teen and in my early twenties, I used to believe that you would only find love or a relationship with someone who was exactly the same as you. Someone who liked all the same things such as music and films, someone who had the same opinion on things, basically someone who was a carbon copy of you with the only difference (if you are heterosexual) being gender. I thought for so long that I struggled in relationships because I was very different from most. I didn't follow fashion or trends, wasn't into pop culture or whatever music was popular. I knew it wasn't impossible but always thought, *Where am I going to find an attractive girl who's into metal music, Tarantino films and enjoys going to the gym as well?*

But as I have matured, I've realised that you don't necessarily have to be exactly the same, and it's not just in loving relationships where this is the case either. I've got a great variety of friends that I get along with so well, and we ourselves vary just as much too. I love Pantera, Motorhead and Slayer whereas a lot of my friends don't, even some of my friends that like metal music don't like these bands. I've got friends I could go to the gym with and some that are more likely to tell me to go and die if I asked them to come with me, but we still get along. Even with love, obviously, if you have a lot in common, then it's going to be a massive help, but if you can get on brilliantly and make a compromise here and there because you love them, then that will also help massively.

So the point I'm making is that it's not a necessity to have everything in common to be close to someone, but you do tend to get closer to those that you do have more in common with. Losing touch with some of my friends that went to university has shown me this as a lot of their closest friends are the friends they made at university because they had similar middle-class upbringings and were doing the same courses. This isn't to say that we can't still be friends as I am still in touch with some of them, but I have drifted away from some of them as well. But the friends I'm closest with now I've known longer than my school friends; they are similar to me in more ways than some of my school friends ever were, and they are now the friends I can trust and rely upon without a moment's thought.

What I am trying to say here is that although we all go through different things in life, and as hard as it may seem, friends will come and go. But the important thing is that the right friends, the right people, will come into your life at the right time. You don't have to try to get them or necessarily force it. In my experience, friends have appeared without me trying and without me realising how much I did actually need them.

The thing we need to know, though, is how we can identify "the right people". People often say that they find it hard to trust others, usually when it comes to relationships, but now more than ever is when it has probably been the toughest time to trust people. Strangely, though, I feel that it has become the simplest time to see when someone is really there for you and does actually care for you. Unsurprisingly, this is no doubt due to the fact that mental health issues are probably at their highest, and we need our friends more than ever.

Most of my friends are from Lichfield, and I've usually lived on the outskirts of Lichfield, so I'll go and see them more than they'll come to me. But as it's usually to go out or to drink, they will, more often than not, offer for me to stay over rather than paying for taxis home. So many times, friends have picked me up or dropped me home, even when I tell them I don't mind driving to them. We buy each other drinks without having to ask or seeing whose round it is. Because these are real friends, we do things without looking for favours in return. We know these people are so good that we do it out of kindness, and they do the same to return that kindness. We know they've done so much for us, and we want to do so much for them.

And though with these gestures, we can often feel indebted to do something nice for them when they do it for us, it's not always the case. We don't always have to wait for a kind act; quite often, it can also be the opposite, and we see it when something bad happens. I've had lots of help from my friends in the past, and as I've said, depression can be something you don't properly understand until you go through it yourself. This is why I will quite often, every few days, just drop a friend a message asking how things are. I do it because when I've struggled in my darkest times, I knew I would have loved for someone to ask me if I was OK rather than having someone say that they'd be there if I needed them.

When people are struggling with mental health, a lot of times people can be quiet or reserved and don't want to open up about what it is that they're going through. But if you can be that person who makes the first move, the person who starts the conversation and asks the question, it can show that you are interested and you want to know that this person is OK. It shows that you care and show consideration without being called upon or forced into doing so. Obviously, you don't want to keep asking all the time and pester them, but if you do it often enough, it can build a deeper trust with people, and when things do go wrong, you could be the first person that they go to for help with whatever the situation may be.

Sometimes, when we have "the right people" in our lives, they can be a bit more nonchalant with how they help us out when we are in times of need. Quite a few times in the past if I've posted something negative on Facebook, whether it's a bad day at work or maybe a break-up, I'll get a text from a mate with quite possibly the simplest method to offer stress relief there is... "Pub?"

Once there, they might tip-toe around what's happened to begin with, but eventually, the negative subject will arise, and your mates will always make you feel better without having to try too hard. Usually, this will be because your focus is on all the negatives, and they will show you all the positive possibilities that could come from this. Doesn't matter how many times this might happen; they will always make you better because they know there will be a time that comes when you will do the same for them.

Occasionally, and this is something that happened to me quite recently, you may not even mention the negative issue at all. As I'm sure many of you are as well, I'm in a group chat. This one, in particular, is with a group of lads, and my best mate told us that he and his girlfriend had split up. I won't go into detail, but an ex was the problem. We gave him our support and told him we'd help him through as any good friend would. But as we showed our support, we also carried on as we normally would. This isn't to say that we just said, "Cheer up, mate," and moved on, but we joked and made fun of each other as if nothing had happened. We obviously didn't make fun of our friend whose girlfriend had split up with him, we're not that harsh, but even he said that the joking and laughs put a smile back on his face and was taking his mind off it. This just shows that though it may not seem like it on the face of things, the right people will always be there and help you through anything, even without being straight and direct to the matter in hand.

So the main subject matter in this chapter is that the right people tend to enter your lives at the right time. They will be there to help you through anything without being asked or called upon. But this doesn't mean that you can just coast through life and they'll automatically be there. This should be one of the earliest sayings that we learn: "Treat people how you want to be treated." The right people will be there for you because you have been there for them. They help without being asked because it's how you have helped them.

Don't just help people to look for something in return, do it to help the relationship you already have. Another great saying you should know is, "It's nice to be nice," and it is. It's one of the major reasons that I'm writing this book: to help others with mental health issues. When I was a personal trainer, I loved it on a weigh-in day when someone had lost weight because it made me feel so good to see how great it had made them feel. Plus, you never know, what doesn't look like much or may seem like something simple to you could mean the absolute world to someone else. With one simple gesture, you could bring another great person into your life and, they could, later on, become another of these "right people" that you are so thankful to have there for you.

I think that at some point in our lives we all experience bad times or negative issues. If we have someone there who is willing to help us through thick and thin, it will be a massive help. Though we may all go through bad situations at some point, I believe it will only be a small percentage of our whole lives, and we will have more positive experiences than negative. In these times, remember to use this positive energy to help those who have helped you and continue to help you but also to offer kindness and goodness to others who need it. You never know what you may accomplish or achieve, and you may even better yourself. Look back at those who have had the biggest influence or have helped you so much in your life and remember to thank them and show the appreciation that you have for them.

Chapter 10
It's Only a Mistake If Nothing Is Learnt

So many of us are so quick to put ourselves down. There are beautiful people out there who think that they are hideous, slim people who think they are fat; we all have our own insecurities. But in this day and age, we are very quick to say that we have done something wrong, made a mistake, and we are so quick to blame ourselves for it. I think that we have to realise that while a mistake can feel bad at the time, it doesn't always mean it's going to cause bad things to happen to us or make them constantly happen.

One of the biggest lessons in life that I have learnt has been that mistakes can help you do better and to better yourself in the future. This can only be the case, though, if we look into these so-called mistakes and realise why they are mistakes, pinpoint where we have gone wrong and what has caused us to do so. I feel like in the times we currently live in and in the last decade or so, as soon as we do something wrong that affects us, we instantly think negatively. Whatever happened has caused something bad to occur at that time or afterwards, so that must mean it is wrong, and we can't look or think about it ever again in case something goes wrong again.

When someone has worked in a trade or for a particular company for longer than someone else, they are often seen as being a better worker in that trade or company. That's because with experience comes knowledge. This means that even though the mistake may have caused negativity, if a situation arises again where something similar happens, then we have the experience to look at it differently and make sure we handle it better and come out with a better result.

I know a lot of that may seem obvious, and people will say hindsight is a wonderful thing, but I just feel like there are too many people who will either give up or blame themselves, and they will then start to feel sorry for themselves. Again, as I've said before, it is OK not to be OK once in a while, but if you keep blaming yourself, then you'll never get anywhere other than feeling lower and lower. Life isn't perfect, and mistakes will happen. I know this is probably the cheesiest saying out there, but that's why they put rubbers on pencils. The moment you can understand the mistake is the moment you can start to make things better for yourself.

Like I've been saying here, a lot of times when a mistake is made, often people will just stop what they're doing and give up. You need to realise that whatever it is you are doing, whether you want to become an athlete, start your own business or create a new invention, if you succeed on your first attempt, then you will be extremely lucky beyond belief. As mentioned previously, experience brings knowledge, and those who have become successful on their chosen path have gained a whole load of experience to get them where they want to be.

In football, footballers are awarded the FIFA World Player of the Year award for being the best player of the year, but the Ballon d'Or (Golden Ball) award is seen as the most prestigious. Cristiano Ronaldo signed for Manchester United at eighteen years old, but he didn't win his first Ballon d'Or until he was twenty-three, in 2008. Unfortunately for Cristiano, Lionel Messi came along not long after and won the next four awards in a row. Ronaldo had to up his game, train harder and become a better-rounded player. Luckily, it paid off, and he won the next two Ballon d'Or awards after Messi in 2013 and 2014 and has won five in total to this day (2020).

This shows that Ronaldo, like the rest of us, has made some mistakes and underestimated things in his life. But he didn't stop playing, didn't tell himself that he wasn't good enough. Every time he lost the Ballon d'Or to Messi, he was coming in second place, but he didn't just say that will do or that's good enough. He went back to the drawing board and looked at what he was doing and where he could improve. How he was training, how he could improve both physically and nutritionally. At the time of writing, Cristiano is thirty-five years old. Most footballers at this age are coming to the end of their careers or have already retired, whereas Ronaldo is not only considered one of the best players in the world, but one of, if not the greatest player to have ever played the game.

It's examples in life like this that show us that we need to be willing to take chances, take risks and not be afraid in life. I know that's a lot easier said than done, but as I've said many times, if you don't ask, you don't get. Every once in a while, in our lifetime, we need to be humbled. There are so many different things that need to be mixed up or changed around to keep them on the right track and to keep them interesting. This is why arguing in a relationship isn't always a bad thing. It can show us what we are doing wrong and where we can improve the relationship to make things better. Obviously, it's not great if every conversation is an argument and you're at each other's throats all the time, but if you see the issue, then you can fix it.

Not only in relationships will you find that things have to get changed up once in a while for them to keep having a positive effect. Having been a former personal trainer, I used to have all kinds of clients come to me for help and advice on their fitness. A lot of times I would get beginners who have never really trained. Sometimes I would get those who trained brilliantly but couldn't control their nutrition properly and some who just wanted to do something new to make a new hobby out of it. But quite often, usually with guys in their late teens to early twenties, they just needed to change their workouts. This could be either increasing the intensity, changing the particular exercise, or even just changing the order of the exercises that they did. The body will eventually get used to the workout that you are doing, and you will have to shock the muscles for them to keep building and progressing in whatever your fitness goals may be.

Fitness goals are great things to have; they are what keep us motivated and give us that drive to continue with our training. But I think that we need to look into the other aspects of our lives and make some goals for those as well. As I've just said, goals will keep you motivated and keep you going. If you don't have any, then things can start to get stale, and you will find that you are not really going anywhere in many places of your life.

I've spoken about it a number of times in this book, but I think one of the biggest places in our lives where this is probably most apparent is within the workplace and in our careers. I think if you were to ask the average person, I don't think they would say that they enjoy their work. Believe me, there are those who love what they do and wouldn't change it for the world, but I think a lot of people have the career that they do for one of two reasons. The first being that the job they have is covering their bills, or they got their job through a family member. These were pretty much the exact reasons why I started off in carpentry. I had to work through college, but it was my dad who initially got me the job at the company that I started working for.

As has been previously mentioned, a lot of people are afraid to go for a job that they want to do or would enjoy because they are afraid that they are not up to the work that is needed to be able to do it, and this probably includes the fear of making mistakes. I'm not saying this is the case for everyone, but I imagine it might be for a lot of them. This is something that I have feared in the past, but it's also something that I eventually went on and did when I became a personal trainer, and looking back, I question myself as to why I was worried about doing it. Why fear something if you don't know what it involves or why fear something that you have never attempted before. If you never try, you'll never know.

Also, even if you were to make a mistake on your way to getting the qualifications that you need, it's not like that will mean you can never have another go at it. If you were to fail one of the exams, you might have to pay again to re-take it, but I'm sure the exam board would still allow you to take the exam again at some point. We are far too quick to jump to the negative aspects of a situation. I'm pretty sure there are those out there who absolutely despise the job that they are in with a passion, but if they took the risk to get into another career, they fear that everything they already have may fall before them, and they would lose it all.

We need to learn to take the occasional risks in life. It will make your life much more interesting and increase the chance of opportunities coming to you. Just think, if every offer you get in life, you choose to play it safe and stick with what you have, nothing will ever improve, and nothing will ever become more exciting. Of course, if you're a millionaire and have everything you ever wanted, then this might be a better option to stick with what you have, but surely, if not, then we will want some more opportunities in life.

If we can set more goals, then we can keep ourselves motivated more often, but we need to make sure that we are willing to work for these goals. There are some people out there who stick with the job they have because it works for them time-wise. But you do sometimes see these being the first people who wish they made more money or are jealous of people in higher positions because they have more. The difference is that they were willing to work for it and put more time in for it.

There are a lot of people in today's world who don't want to work as hard but want the benefits that come with working hard. Some aren't willing to change their position in their current career or change job completely because it may mean more hours or more travelling. They may feel that they've made a mistake somewhere in life, which means they don't make as much pay, but they don't want the chance to improve it. I understand if you are happy with what you do, but you can't moan at your situation if you don't take the chances that you get, and this is what I mean by saying it will only be a mistake if you don't learn from it.

Albert King was an American blues guitarist and singer that had a song that described this kind of attitude perfectly, and that was called "Everybody wants to go to heaven, but nobody wants to die." Basically, this means that if you want the rewards in life, if you want to make life better, then you must be willing to work for these rewards. If we just want to try to coast through our lives, then we won't get anywhere. We may make mistakes and miss opportunities that are presented to us. I know we all have our own opinions, and sometimes we feel worse about our situations than others would, but one thing that has helped me on a few occasions is that when things are at their hardest and things feel impossible, I remember that there is always someone who is going through something worse and those who have made it through worse. This means that no matter how bad things may seem or may get, we will all be able to get through them eventually.

I can remember one month in particular when I was feeling pretty down about the seizures I was having. I had two in just less than two weeks, and for the first time, I had aspirated during one of them. A couple of days later, I went to the hospital and was told that the chest x-ray I had was showing that I may have coronavirus. Having watched the news a lot and hearing that people with pre-existing conditions tend to have a weaker immune system compared to those without any conditions and were quite high on the risk scale when it came to fatalities due to coronavirus, I was starting to overthink things and was starting to think the worst because I'm diabetic.

One night my mum was watching the *Celebrity Great British Bake Off* for Stand Up To Cancer. I came downstairs and started watching it too. Just before the advert breaks, they would show a story about someone who had dealt with cancer. The story on this particular break was about a young couple in their early thirties. They had three young daughters, all under five. The father was diagnosed but was also cured of his cancer. Unfortunately, it had returned a year later and, sadly, he didn't pull through. He was only around thirty-four and seemed like a normal, fit and healthy guy.

At first, it was something that really hit me hard. I thought if someone in good shape like him and only in his early thirties could so easily pass, then maybe I could as well. But as the story progressed, I started to feel better too. I was worrying for his wife because she was still young and had three young daughters to raise on her own, plus they had to live without a father. I started to think that they must be having a much worse time than me, so I questioned why I was getting so worked up. But then, as I continued to watch, the story showed pictures of them smiling and then showed them today, a few years older. They were still smiling, and though the girls said they missed their dad, they also said how proud they were of him, as did his wife. From then, all I could think was, *Well, if they can get through something as horrible as that, then my issues shouldn't be a problem.*

I think that something that we all need to realise in our lives is that not every moment is going to be a good one. It's not going to be full of success or accomplishments. But also, I think we need to realise that something that makes our lives that much more exciting is that the clock is ticking and at some point, it will all come to an end. I used to have a mindset similar to that of an athlete, thinking that I had to achieve everything I wanted before I reached my mid-thirties. I must be married and have my own house before then, but now I see that's not the case.

We won't be young or in peak condition forever, so let's make the most of the time that we do have and do it as often as we can. Let's not stop once we reach the top or achieve our goals; keep pushing forward and make new goals, new targets so we can keep our lives interesting and not one day look back and think we've made a mistake somewhere. Don't be afraid to challenge yourself when it comes to setting your goals either; remember that the harder it may be, the greater the reward will be once you achieve it. Even if you have made a mistake or two in life, try to learn from them and allow them to help you in the future.

As I'm writing this chapter, we are in lockdown because of coronavirus. Sure, there are those who say they hate it or they're bored of all of this but use this time wisely. A lot of us will have time that we have never had before or thought we would get. Use any unexpected available time to do things that you've always wanted to do but always said, "Oh, I'll never have the time to get that chance." Why do you think I'm currently writing this book! Normally, I would be working nine hours a day, but now I have the time. Those who say they can't get in shape or have no time to go to the gym try to use this time now to do so. As the chapter suggests, there's nothing wrong with making a mistake or two in life, as long as we learn from them and use them to help us in the future.

Chapter 11
Painful Lessons That Have Been Learnt

The feelings of anxiety and depression are not quite the same as when you feel physical feelings of trauma or pain. They are not just something that you one day wake up with or just suddenly start to feel. It's not like one day you feel fine, and then all of a sudden, you start to lose confidence in yourself, or you start to feel negative about every feeling that you have. In life, we all have different experiences and experience the same things others have but in a variety of different ways.

In my experience, I've always felt that I was more depressed than I was anxious. For me, the road to depression was a slow path of realisation, and by this I mean, that it took me a while to realise and come to terms with the fact that I may be suffering with depression. Like I said in the opening of this paragraph, there wasn't necessarily a specific day or event that suddenly just made me feel really down about everything; it slowly built up until, eventually, I had to basically stop and ask myself, *Do I have depression?*

These types of questions were initially starting while I was at work in the building trade as a carpenter; I started to think that this was where I spent the majority of my time and where I had the most time to myself to think. Most of the time, anything I had to moan about was work-related, and it was where I had the most time to overthink things before, I really understood what overthinking was. On my breaks, I would usually just be sitting in my car looking on social media and seeing all the things friends were achieving that I wasn't. The more and more I was in this cycle, the more I would start to question myself.

Things really picked up once I had qualified as a personal trainer, but there were also a lot of other things I had to learn from this as well. It wasn't until about a year before I decided to end being a trainer that I really started to think that I was truly depressed and that I needed to start looking into what kinds of help were available. The fact that I had achieved such a massive goal by getting a dream job that I wanted to do was amazing. Turning one of my hobbies into a career had made me feel absolutely fantastic. The problems that I had been having, though, were that I had been jumping to conclusions and making assumptions about this career. In my mind and many other people's minds, personal trainers were raking in the money. Also, before I had started the course I needed to complete to become qualified, I had no idea about the facts and details about being self-employed. There were so many points that I hadn't given a second thought to when I decided to become qualified.

I had no idea that if I wanted to work in a gym that I would have to pay rent regularly to work there. I knew there would be other trainers there, but I never realised how difficult it would be to get and keep clients once they started training with me. Eventually, it got to the point that it felt like I was paying the gym to allow me to work there. In my mind, I had just thought I'd moved into a much higher paying career and one that I was going to enjoy a whole lot more.

Unfortunately, there have been far too many times that I just thought something was going to happen or those things would just improve. As I've previously spoken about in this book, I had always thought that the older I got and the longer that I stayed in a job, that my pay would naturally rise over time. I was always one to think that I'd just succeed, I didn't really need to think about it, and it would just happen in its own time. But as the years kept clocking by and less and less happened, the more that doubt started to creep in and the worse I was starting to feel. I know I've said the fear of failure was my biggest fear but, at this point, it was the fear of the unknown that was really starting to get to me.

There were just constant unknown answers to questions about the future: Would I ever get onto the property ladder? Would I ever start a family of my own? Would this be a career for the rest of my days? While these may be questions that I do still sometimes ask myself, it has been one of the many lessons that I have had to learn in my young adult life, along with quite a few others. They are not the nicest lessons to learn, but I must admit to you all, I am very thankful that I have learnt these harsh lessons as, without these, I wouldn't be able to progress as far as I would wish to in my lifetime.

As I was growing up and progressing in life, I saw so many different aspects of life in a different way. Throughout my life, I had seen so many of my friends and family just kind of sail through. They'd get their careers going, find their love interests, buy a house together and start families. Because I was in that same family and same circle of friends, I just thought it would happen at some point. In terms of being in my late twenties, still single, and still in one of my parents' houses, it was like hearing about illnesses on the news like foot and mouth or bird flu... it will never happen to me.

But here I am, writing this at twenty-eight years old and living in my mother's house.

This is without a doubt the biggest lesson that I have learnt throughout my young life, and that is to be careful not to misjudge life. Just because something is common and you've never seen bad things happen to anyone that you know doesn't mean that they won't happen to you. In my teen imagination, at twenty-eight years old, I should be in my own house with my lovely wife and maybe a child or two, perhaps thinking about a holiday. But as I've made very clear, sometimes things don't go how you expect, and they certainly don't always go how you want them to.

Going back to the occupational world, I think that whether we are in the jobs we dreamt of as kids or even absolute billionaires, every job will have some aspect of it that we didn't expect until we start it. Jobs are immensely important to us, obviously because they support us financially, but I think that they affect us physically and mentally as well. As I've already brought up a number of times, it was my job that initially got me started on my path to depression, and I think this can and will have happened to millions of people all over the world. If we don't get into something we want to do or something that will support us enough, then it can be a certain road to disaster.

Like I pointed out in the previous paragraph, even amazing jobs will have aspects that people didn't think about before starting them. I'm sure a lot of men dream of becoming footballers, playing football as work you get paid thousands of pounds a week — sounds brilliant. But you have to keep a watch on your diet at all times; you have to watch what you say and do in case the media gets hold of it and makes a story. If you're seen in public, you won't get left alone by the public asking for photos and autographs. You've got to remember, though: all of this is only if you do make it to a top league.

Just imagine, you've been involved in a sport since you were about eight. You went to training multiple times a week, played games all the time. Stayed in the best possible shape you could by keeping an eye on nutrition regularly. You didn't go to university or college because you were already in a team youth academy, and when you get to seventeen or eighteen years old, they turn around and tell you that you're not good enough and you're not what they're looking for. You may be able to carry on for a lesser club but, with all that time and work that you have put in to try to achieve your dreams, you would be devastated.

But it's not just in the celebrity world where you could be misled, though. When I became a carpenter, I thought it was brilliant. I'd got a great trade behind me, people will always need a carpenter, and I was making a decent wage. What I didn't think about was how much time I would be working away and staying in hotels in places that I didn't know. I didn't know about shortages of work and being laid off because sometimes there wouldn't always be enough work to go around to keep everyone on.

It was similar to when I became a personal trainer. I thought it was a dream come true — what I did as a hobby was now my career. This was, of course, before I realised it's a lot harder than it seems to get new clients. You may find that you do more time travelling than you do actually working. Self-employment does have its good points but also comes with a lot of downsides too. I'm sure if you asked everyone that you knew to make a list of pros and cons of their jobs that they could do it very easily without hesitation.

Of course, it isn't just the working world that can lead us into darkness; we can often feel low because we can often feel alone. A lot of my sadness is due to not having achieved what others have achieved or simply not having what others have. I am now at that age where a lot of people I know are getting engaged but more commonly now getting married. My brothers were very lucky to marry the first girls that they fell for, whereas I had many different girlfriends and love interests. I can even remember my oldest brother Ben asking me for advice about girls in his late teens.

I suppose I always thought that one day I would get married, and I still believe that I will, but I always thought it would happen because I had lots of experience with love in the past. The problem is, though, my relationships only last a couple of months or so, and it wasn't until I got deep into my adult years that I really understood why. In my teens, I always had a crush. I'd be massively interested in someone and be a bit of a hopeless romantic when it came down to it. Once I was in my early twenties and having relationships, at the time, I would think that maybe it would go somewhere and that we had things in common. But the short end of it was that either I was moving on from someone I desperately fancied or was moving on from a previous relationship.

Although it isn't a particular lesson in that chapter, if you can learn why particular things have happened or have been going the way they have been, it will without a doubt help you massively in the future. This is the exact point of the previous chapter; mistakes will only be mistakes if you don't learn anything from them; otherwise, you'll keep making that same mistake, which is something that I did. Now that I can see why it has kept happening and why I haven't been able to settle down, perhaps now I can learn from that mistake, and, in the future, I will be able to get myself into a long-lasting relationship and a step closer to the happiness that I've been seeking.

In my mind, your love life is obviously part of your social life, and it is probably the biggest part of your social life. Your working life and your social life are, in my opinion, the two biggest aspects of adult life. By this, I mean that they are your most important aspects and lead to so much more in your life. Without work, we wouldn't have the finances to live, have our homes and experience the world that we know. Without our social life and, more importantly, love life, we could be so stressed beyond belief. To have no one there to believe in you or pick you up when you are down would just be an awful experience.

Throughout this section, I have talked about how I have misjudged the careers that I have had and how I have misjudged the relationships that I have been in. Thinking that they would be different to what they actually were and thinking the relationships ended for different reasons. It's due to these reasons that I have learnt what has ultimately given me the biggest cause for being on a path to depression, and that cause is the feeling of having failed.

I may be repeating certain aspects here, but one of the best lessons you can learn is to know the reason why you feel depressed or have anxiety. Once you start to know that reason, you can start to understand your feelings better, start to see how you can adjust and what you can do to make yourself feel better rather than just continuing to feel sad and sorry for yourself. If you can see what's making you feel so down, then you can try to change those feelings. By continuing to feel sad, you will just continue to follow this dark path and fall lower and lower.

As I have identified, for me, it is the feeling of having failed or being unsuccessful. I see so many people around me who have achieved what I would like to achieve, such as buying a home, meeting "the one" and getting married. Because I haven't achieved things like this, it makes me feel like I'm failing. But now I know that this is what is causing me to feel depressed, I can start to look at my situation from a different perspective as I don't want to be continuously depressed. I can see that some people are brought up in higher classes and financially have more available to them; I shouldn't have anything against them — that's just the luck of the draw. It's because of this, and there have been times where I have experienced it, you will have to work harder and put the extra effort in to get the things you want to achieve, but it feels so much better when you do.

Rather than just being sad or wanting pity from people, I can now look into what I need to do to get to the places that I want to be. I can now set goals or targets, and it's these that give me the motivation to push on with my life and give me much more to remain occupied with rather than just being alone with my thoughts and overthinking myself into a horrible pit of doom. It may not be a quick fix, and these things will take time, but if we never give it a go, then we will never know at all whether it will help us improve.

So for the last couple of chapters, the theme has been the lessons we can learn from our mistakes. Earlier I spoke of how I misjudged the two biggest aspects of adult life: work and social life, which has made me feel like I've failed and ultimately made me depressed. This has made me realise that by having experienced depression and, to be honest, by currently still experiencing parts of it, I have probably no doubt misjudged life, which again is another lesson learnt.

When we are younger, we don't really worry too much about the future; we just tend to think, *Well, it'll happen when it happens*. I know I've brought this up before, but I always thought there were certain ages you need to do things by. I also said something is only a mistake if you don't learn from it. Having gone through depression, I see now that the mistake isn't achieving something by the common age it's usually done by; it's believing that there are certain times that they need to be done by. You have to look back and see what could have been the reason that you haven't achieved something by the time others have. If, like me, it may be that you haven't got that step on the property ladder yet because you took a chance at trying to get into a career that you loved and always wanted rather than being stuck in a nine-to-five job that you despised. You might not yet have met "the one" because maybe you're actually looking for someone you share things with, someone you really enjoy spending time with rather than just settling for anyone who comes knocking or someone with looks that you can show off to your friends.

A lot of us are the type of people that if we feel like we're in a world of doom and gloom, we will be very quick to blame ourselves and say it's our fault. It's OK to feel down once in a while and OK not to be OK, but we also need to look out for ourselves too. I don't mean that we have to be selfish and only look out for ourselves but just not go straight to the negative and look at what we could do to improve our situation. In our younger days, normally, if we had made a mistake, we would instantly regret it and feel horrible. As we get older and wiser, I believe we all have it within ourselves to look back and think, *Without that, I may not have*

learnt a lot of the valuable lessons that I'll need to get
me to where I want to be in the future.

Mistakes aren't always a negative thing, and it isn't always because of us that we are in the positions that we are in. In life, we obviously have a lifespan, but that doesn't mean there are times by which things need to be done. It's OK to not be OK. There might be others out there who are going through or have experienced worse, but this doesn't mean you can't feel down about your situation. Just remember that if you don't learn the reason that you have gotten on to this dark path towards depression or anxiety, then it is very tricky to get off it or change your direction.

Chapter 12
Advice

Like a lot of people who have suffered with anxiety or depression, I often feel that I'm very good at helping those close to me, such as my friends or family who are going through these types of feelings. This is no doubt because, like those who may also feel good at giving advice, I'm not the best at asking for help. What I mean by this is that because I've rarely been one to ask others for help, I tend to suffer in silence and use my own methods to get through hard times. This is why I feel like I'm good at helping others and giving advice because I'm someone who has gone through similar difficulties, and the advice I have given has helped me in the past.

When I talk about not asking for help, it's not because I feel like I'm good enough to get through tough times myself or that I don't need the help; it's more because I don't want to seem weak to others or make people think I'm just looking for attention. My biggest reason, though, is that I sometimes feel that if I ask people for help, then I'm letting that person down or making them feel disappointed in me. Unfortunately, feeling like I have let people down was one of the biggest causes of my depression to begin with.

With this being the case, my first piece of advice to anyone going through these sorts of tough times would be not to be embarrassed or afraid to talk to people about what it is that you are going through. It isn't the simplest of things to do but talking to your family and friends can be a massive help. Your family will always be there for you and can help you with whatever it might be that is causing these troubles. When it comes to your friends, if they are not there for you to help you, are they really a friend? True friends will do anything for you; they won't even have to think about it. If you are going through a hard time, they will help in any way they can and as soon as they can. The issues that are causing you to feel depressed are, no doubt, subjects that you look at in a negative fashion. If you speak to your friends or family about them, chances are they will see them in a different fashion and will be able to reassure you that all is not lost, showing you that there are some pros about these particular issues.

It has been stated many times throughout this book that overthinking is a very horrible thing and can cause a lot of grief. If you keep the issues that are bothering you to yourself, then you are going to be stuck carrying this weight around, and it isn't going to do you any favours. If you are able to sit and discuss the problem with someone, then you may help yourself massively in lifting this weight off your back as they may reassure you or give you the advice you need to get through this difficult period. Sometimes it can even help to speak to someone you don't know. Again, I've mentioned it before, but I've spoken to a mental health doctor in the past; doing this helped and taught me a lot of new things about my mental health. The reason it can help is because you don't know these people like family or a friend. With this being the case, you don't feel as close to them, and you won't feel like you are letting them down or will upset them if you explain to them what's going on and how you are feeling.

One of the other major causes for my depression was the feeling that I'd been failing in certain aspects of life because I hadn't achieved things that many other people my age had done. One thing that helped me was rather than looking at the negatives, to try to look at things from a positive angle. I may not have bought a house or gotten married when others had, but I had taken a risk in my life and got into a career that I enjoyed. Looking for the positive isn't always as simple as it sounds, so, for me, another way to stop looking at the negative side is to write myself a list of goals.

If you write yourself a list of goals that you want to achieve, then this gives you some inspiration, some motivation to push yourself and get yourself going again rather than just feeling down all the time and wishing things had gone differently. As you get older, you realise that you are never too old to do certain things, and life is never too short to achieve your goals. If there are things that you have trouble with in life, a list of goals can help you improve these things by giving you a reason to improve. For example, I've always had difficulty with saving money, but I realise if I ever want to get onto the property ladder, then I have to improve this. This now gives me a purpose, a reason to improve and the motivation to improve my ability to save. Every time I see the list of goals I have written, it reminds me to try to save, and it's something I now do much more often than I used to.

Even though I have written a list of goals, quite recently, following a friend's advice, I have written myself a bucket list as well. For a long time, I was always one who thought that you had to be getting on in life or be quite old before you thought about writing a bucket list, but as I mentioned before, you are never too old. This, again, has given me great inspiration and the motivation to do things. A lot of things on the list involve travelling to places and doing certain things in particular, so, yet again, I now have a reason to save money and do things to help me earn more money.

With a set of goals, you give yourself a set of targets that you want to achieve, but, more than that, you give yourself things to think about other than whatever the issues are that are causing you to feel down. If you always think about the negative aspects of life or the issues causing you to feel anxious or depressed, then that's how you are always going to be. Keep yourself busy and occupied. Obviously, we all need time for ourselves and time to rest, but don't give yourself time to always be overthinking things or thinking about the worst possibilities.

Whenever we overthink something, we usually think negatively. We'll usually think, *But what if this happens?* Or *What if I'm not good enough?* We need to realise that anything in life that's worth having will never come easy. Before you get a job and start earning money, you have to go through at least twelve years of school and, depending on what career path you want to take, the education process won't end there. Rewards don't come easy, and they won't come overnight, it's going to take hard work and effort, but you will feel so much better for putting that hard work and effort into the things that you do.

There are some things that I don't necessarily regret but that I wish that I had done differently. I wish I wasn't as shy when I started secondary school and got into rugby sooner than I did. Who knows how successful I could have been, but that doesn't mean I've run out of time. I could still join rugby clubs and play; I even joined one when I left school, and it was brilliant, improved my fitness, and I met lots of great new people. This just goes to show what you could achieve if you set yourself some new goals. You never know what new things may happen in your life if you meet new people or start new hobbies. You could perhaps end up getting new job opportunities or, if you are single, could even meet that certain someone.

The most important thing is that you could keep yourself occupied and forget about all the troubles that were bringing you down. Feel more positive and have a more enjoyable lifestyle. Find yourself having better and more productive sleep which will make you feel better and healthier. No more are you constantly thinking "what if" or so negatively all the time, but instead, you just go for it. Having a set of goals will help you to be more productive and outgoing, and it will be because of this that you now enjoy your life a whole lot more than what it used to be.

But before any of this can happen, we need to look at ourselves and look at what we need to do. We need to see where we need help and what we will have to do to get it. While I've said that it's OK to ask others for help, like I've also said, we also need to see the work and effort that we need to put in to help ourselves. We can't just sit back and rely on others to do everything for us and just fix it all like that. There's no point in just sitting back and hoping everyone will feel sorry for us because that isn't going to fix it either.

It's OK not to be OK, but if we just stick with our negative attitudes and mope around all the time, eventually people will leave us to it. They won't want to hang around with you because they'll just think you're miserable all the time, and that doesn't make things fun or exciting. If you can show them that deep down, even through the hard times, you still have some inner strength and wisdom to help you get out of the difficult times, they will still have tonnes of respect for you. It is with that respect that when the time comes, and you need it the most, they will offer that helping hand without you even asking for it. Having so much care and respect for you will mean they want to keep that person they care for around rather than having someone going through dreadful times, and not being the same person they know and care for.

Mental health is a very tricky subject to deal with, but luckily, nowadays, it is out in the open more than ever with so many different resources to help us through. We all have different experiences with mental health, but I feel like I have ups and downs with it; some weeks will be good, and sometimes they can bring me down again. I feel that one of the biggest lessons to learn that can help you through the difficult times is that you can understand your mental health much better when you get a better understanding of life.

By this, I mean that life itself can be a hard experience and a tough challenge. But that doesn't mean that we can't enjoy our lives or it can't be fun and, as I've mentioned a few times while writing this, the harder something is, the greater the reward can be. It's this type of mindset that can give us the motivation and inspiration to push on with our lives and try to get the best out of them that we can. We will always have the time to achieve things, and it will never be too late for us just as long as we keep putting in the hard work and effort that we need to get the most rewarding experiences that we know are out there.

What we need to remember is that we are not in this on our own, and we are not the only ones who go through bad times. It's OK to have bad days but, more importantly, it's OK to ask for help from others if we need it on those bad days. Try to stay in a positive frame of mind whenever it's possible. If all we do to try to sort these negative situations out is think about how they could get more negative, then that is what they will do. I know this may annoy a lot of people, but probably the biggest piece of advice I can give is that we all need to have some patience as well. I may not be the most tolerant person myself or have the longest fuse, but I also know that not everything can be fixed or solved overnight. If you can understand this too, you will already be starting to win your battle.

Chapter 13
The Writing Experience

I can quite honestly say that writing this book has been the toughest challenge that I have ever attempted. I have definitely underestimated how long this was going to take me to write, but I think I also underestimated the subject material too. This is the first book that I've ever written and obviously doing anything for the first time is going to be a challenge, but when it's about something so personal and close to my own emotions, it just made it that much harder.

That isn't to say that I haven't enjoyed the writing experience, but it did bring back some dark times and made me re-live some difficult periods that have happened recently in my lifetime. But at the same time, writing about them has been my version of talking about them and has really helped me feel better about things. There are still some challenges for me to go through and things I want to accomplish but writing about my emotions has made me much more comfortable talking about them, and this should do so much for me in the future.

It has shown me which things about myself that I need to work on and also helped me learn what I need to do to take care of those particular things. This in itself shows that I'm not just writing for the sake of it but shows I can take the advice that I'm giving to help with my own mental health. Just the experience of writing this book has not only helped me feel better in myself, but it also feels like I have gotten a lot off my chest.

Just the time and practice that I have had in writing this book has given me a much greater understanding of the reasons why I have felt depressed or have felt the effects of anxiety. Having to write out the emotions and experiences that I have gone through and then reading through them all to double-check them almost made me feel as if I were experiencing them again. It's been a great way to help myself through any difficult periods because rather than speaking to somebody else or a stranger about it, it feels as if I have discussed it with myself and can see the reasons for my depression and anxiety much clearer than I once did.

But it hasn't just been my feelings that I have managed to get a better understanding of. It has also helped with some of the pieces of advice that I have included throughout this book. Yet again, rather than just talking to someone, trying to help them and give them pieces of help and advice, I've had to write them out and read them to double-check they're right. Seeing and reading them multiple times made me appreciate them much more. With this being the case, it allows me to use these helpful tips much more and allows me to help my own situation a lot more than I would have in the past.

Although writing the book has been a challenge for me and has been a massive help to me with my own mental health, the thing that it has probably helped me with the most is the timing of the writing. I have been writing this throughout 2020 and the peak of the global Covid-19 pandemic. Now, obviously, throughout this time, my country (UK) has been in lockdown and, for a time, people weren't allowed to work, but I had been like this for five months before lockdown due to different medical reasons. I have also not been allowed to drive anywhere, and we've had to keep social distancing rules in place.

With all of this being the case, writing this book has also massively helped me get through this tough time. It has helped me keep my mind focused and has kept me occupied on an objective, which has been one of the biggest and most consistently mentioned pieces of advice that I have written in this book to help you with difficult periods of mental health. This just goes to show that if you do ever get lost in your own thoughts and start overthinking about dark or negative things, if you find something to keep your mind focused and especially something that will lead you to complete a goal, you can find yourself thinking more positively and working towards a brighter path.

I've probably no doubt already mentioned it whilst writing, but a major goal of mine of writing the book is to not only help those who are struggling with their mental health but to motivate and inspire those who are struggling. There have been many people that I've known who have gone through or are going through dark times in their lives, and they tend to stick with the negative aspects of it. There's nothing wrong with having bad days from time to time; I still have them occasionally. But the kind of people I'm talking about are the ones where every social media post is a dark picture or a sad sentence. Again, it's OK not to be OK, but moping around or feeling sorry for yourself all day every day is not going to help or get you any further.

There has to be a time at some point where you get sick of being down, when you don't want to be angry any more, and you say to yourself, *You know what? I'm going to get up and make something of myself.* I hope that in this book, there is more than just the odd paragraph that can do that for readers. Pieces of advice and stories that I've shared can show other people that have been through rough times that this doesn't necessarily mean you can't amount to anything. You don't have to be a certain age, certain race or gender to achieve something, nor is there any particular deadline for you to meet. As long as you are qualified, determined and willing to put the time in, then you have every chance of succeeding.

With this being a strong belief of mine, what writing this book has done for me is to remind me to take some chances in my life, make some opportunities of my own. I feel that far too often in our lives, and this is something that I've certainly been guilty of myself, we stand around and wait for these opportunities and chances in our lives to just present themselves, and we hope they come out of the blue.

We can often think, *People win the lottery all the time; maybe if I buy a ticket, then this week will be my week.* Usually when we think of these types of things, we think of things that won't take much work, or we won't have to do much. Sometimes we can even think of simple things like this but still just not get round to them because we just don't have the confidence to do so, something like perhaps going on a game show. A lot of times we may hear people who moan about their life situation or moan that they wish they had more money but don't do anything to help improve their situation. I can understand if certain circumstances may have caused issues that may not allow you to do certain things, such as medical issues, but you can still research or look into what you may be able to do to get around these issues that could help.

If you look into professional footballers' careers, more often than not, they say they started playing before they reached double figures in age. They will mention that they joined a professional club academy before they reached their teens. If they have the desire, motivation and are passionate about the sport, then they will do all they can and do whatever it takes to keep playing and get a regular spot in the first team, even if that means switching clubs to get more experience or a better chance of playing.

The point of this is that within the time from joining their first team as a child to playing regularly at a professional club, they will have trained hard and put so much time and effort in to get to where they are today. It just goes to show that if you do put the time and the work in, there is no telling how far you may go, but you have to be willing to take the chance. A lot of times, if other people suggest doing things, then they will knock the idea back or doubt themselves straight away. When I first suggested the idea to myself about writing this book, it was only because I knew I would have a lot of spare time. But pretty much straight after I thought of it, I said to myself, *Yeah, but I doubt anyone will publish it. I've never written a book in my life.*

If you ever find yourself in a situation like this, you need to try to build up your confidence and start thinking positively about it. Many guys out there will know what I mean when I speak about asking out a girl they like; you do it because you really like them and want them really bad. In these cases, even if you think she's out of your league and you doubt yourself, chances are you will still ask her out because of how much you want to be with them. It's these types of thoughts that you need to have if you ever doubt yourself when it comes to trying something new or something that could help you. The odds might be against me, but if I never try it, then I will never know.

Like I said, writing this book has reminded me to take some chances in life and create some opportunities of my own. It's done what several things have done in the past, and it's got me overthinking, but this time it's got me overthinking in a positive way. As I've just spoken about, yes, I've thought that it would be doubtful that my book would get published, but I've also thought about if it does get published. How successful could this be if it does? Could this even be the start of a new career for me? Just think that if all the answers to these thoughts were positive, how great the future could be. And all of that would have come from putting in the time and effort into trying something new, to have the motivation to take a risk and to have the belief in yourself that you can achieve something great.

Obviously, I'm hoping that I can be successful in writing this book, but whether or not this book is successful and is published, the writing experience has taught me a lot more than I thought it would. Even if it doesn't get published, the process has taught me to have more confidence in myself and to not only try more things but to have a wider variety of things that I do try. I've learnt not to worry so much about the outcome and be so quick to knock back an idea because I may discover something new that I enjoy or something I want to learn more about.

The subject of this book is anxiety and depression and ways to deal with it; the writing itself could even be considered to be a few of those ways. As I cited in previous chapters, it has kept me focused, so I've got something productive to look into. It has kept me occupied and busy so I don't find myself overthinking about different negative issues. And probably the best thing that writing this has done for me is to give me some goals, targets to aim for, and these, in particular, are what have kept me focused.

I have already said how one of my most important goals in writing this book was to hopefully help others who are going through difficult times with their mental health and to help them improve it. If I can already do something that has covered some of the topics I've mentioned and something that has helped me to improve my own mental health, chances are that this could be a positive aid to others, and I really hope it can be. If this was to be successful and help those who are going through tough times right now, then it would be nothing but an honour for me to know that I have been able to help you through. Thank you for looking into my story, and I hope I have been able to give you some helpful advice.